Praise for *HIT IT OFF*

"Joe Brocato's *HIT IT OFF* is a must-read book, packed with compelling scientific research and practical, real-world stories. His 21 Rules will allow readers to hit it off with everyone they meet and develop unique, lasting personal and business relationships."

—Keith Ferrazzi
#1 *New York Times* best-selling author of *Never Eat Alone, Who's Got Your Back,* and *Leading Without Authority*

"*HIT IT OFF* reminds me of a beautifully written song that includes all the essential elements of success. Joe Brocato's 21 Rules are like a catchy melody that you'll always remember. The rhythm of how Joe presents each Rule and the science that backs it up will inspire you. And the overall feeling of the book will motivate you to look at relationships with others in a more conscious way. Joe's written a No. 1 hit here!"

—Jim Peterik
Songwriter and musician
Cowriter of the Grammy Award-winning song "Eye of the Tiger," theme song for *Rocky III*

"Our enduring desire as human beings is to belong—to be deeply connected—to know that we are valued! Joe's concise, researched guidelines will assure that you create an ambience in your relationships where others are visible, heard, and validated! They will come back to you for business! They will stay with you for life!"

—Cher A. Geiger
Psy.D. Licensed clinical psychologist

"As a strategic communications consultant for high-performing CEOs and executive management teams, I am particularly cognizant of the fact that interpersonal and communication skills are necessary for maximum impact and influence. *HIT IT OFF*'s 21 Rules home in on the essence of these skills and will empower you to maximize your personal and professional goals!"

—Jennifer Wojan
CEO/Founder, Capture Communications Group

"One of the key components to success is building relationships. Some people are born with a natural curiosity and the gift of gab. Others struggle when it comes to sparking and keeping a conversation going. Whichever you are, the 21 Rules in Joe's book will make a huge difference, not just in your professional life, but in your personal one as well. The world revolves around people and relationships. Read *HIT IT OFF* and build a better you!"

—Andrew D. Pitcairn
Chair/Director, Pitcairn Family Council

"From my first meeting with Joe, I knew that I wanted to be a client of his. He's smart and savvy with excellent people skills. *HIT IT OFF* embodies his insightful perspective on relationships, with the bonus of terrific personal anecdotes."

—Victoria Sopik
CEO, Kids & Company (Toronto)

"Even after a professional football career and 27 years in the insurance and investment business, I've never seen all these important relationship-building concepts in one place, backed by science. Joe Brocato's *HIT IT OFF* is your own personal game plan around important people skills. Joe's engaging style reminds me of a perfect spiral connecting quarterback and receiver, as they partner toward a touchdown. This book will make a great holiday gift for my adult children and everyone in my network! Absolutely loved it!"

—Brent Novoselsky
ChFC® Former professional football player, Chicago Bears and Minnesota Vikings, and investment management professional

"In the world of executive talent, building and developing relationships is at the heart of the matter. Joe provides the perfect playbook with a sense of real authenticity and life experience. We can all use a bit of help sometimes in how we are building relationships. This is a great guide, reminder, and educator. *HIT IT OFF* gives something for everybody."

—Andrew Stoneham Knott
CEO, Miramar Global (London)

"In professional services, the ability to develop and maintain deep meaningful relationships is a key factor in being successful and ultimately making partner. Joe Brocato's *HIT IT OFF* gives any aspiring professional 21 key elements—rules—to live by. The practical examples are all relatable and help bring the rules to reality. As a veteran of over 30 years, I also picked up some helpful tips to improve my relationship development."
—Antony Nettleton
Northern Illinois Market Leader and Assurance Practice Leader, Sikich LLP

"As the founder of Forum, a global peer group of principals and experts drawn from the senior echelons of the business community and family offices, I am particularly sensitive to the concept of meaningful relationships among people from around the world. *HIT IT OFF* is a literal map for navigating the essential skills with people you will need to achieve your goals in life and business."
—Simon Jacot de Boinod
Founder, Forum (London)

"Joe Brocato's book *HIT IT OFF* is a succinct extrapolation of and "how to" guide to building lasting business relationships. Without a solid business relationship database, it is difficult to succeed in any endeavor. Joe's distilled playbook on building relationships is a must-read for everyone who values having a deep experiential pool at the ready."
—Tony Beyer
Owner and President, Tek Pak, Inc., and Chicagoland Entrepreneur of the Year

"Working in strategic communication between Asia and the Western world, my goal is to facilitate meaningful connections between people of different cultures. Empathy, trust, and conscious listening are key in order to learn about different viewpoints and create deeper understanding. Meaningful relationships are the foundation for long-lasting opportunities. Joe's experience and *HIT IT OFF*'s 21 Rules will provide great insights and surely help you connect with other people in more meaningful ways."
—Stefan Pellech
CEO/Founder, Sinotan (Mainland China)

"Joe Brocato's *HIT IT OFF* is a direct, clear, and compelling read that dives deep into the essence of what makes business grow and life meaningful—the cultivation of real, deep relationships. For those striving to grow their business or who are curious to connect with others on a deeper level, this is a must-read!"

—Michael Cklamovski
President, Northern California at Northern Trust

"As a career relationship manager and mother of three, Joe's 21 Rules to "hit it off" provide an easy-to-use framework to develop mutually beneficial relationships in business and in life generally. Just like the works of Zig Ziglar and Dale Carnegie, *HIT IT OFF* is a must-read! I'm excited to share this handy guide with my team at work and my family!"

—Laura S. Collins
CCIM Senior Director, Asset Management and Advisory, Westmount Realty Capital

"*HIT IT OFF* reminds us that the best way to build meaningful and long-lasting relationships is to truly care about the other person's success and well-being."

—Jack Downing
Assistant Vice President, Marsh USA, Inc.

"Joe's *HIT IT OFF* is right on point. It's all about building relationships. The longer and deeper, the better. It's about building trust. Good relationships build trust. Following Joe's mantra and listening, you'll find that you don't need to 'sell' services, you'll provide solutions. Many of my business relationships became personal relationships—a deeply rewarding part of life and business."

—Barry M. Masek
CPA Partner Emeritus, Baker Tilly US, LLP and former Illinois Regional Assurance Leader and Sales Leader

"Building really enjoyable and highly profitable business relationships is both an art and a skill. You will find no better guide than Joe Brocato. He has walked his talk, doing this at every level for over thirty hard-earned years.

Follow the nuance and detail to his rules and his genuine love of people, and you will be astonished by the rewards!"

—Matt Anderson
Author of *Fearless Referrals* and President of Breakthrough Bound

"*HIT IT OFF* elevates relationship science to a new level. Joe Brocato uses empathy as a tool to build successful business relationships."

—Caren Yanis
Principal, Croland Consulting, LLC

"If you are fascinated by life's unstated rules, want to elevate your game, and feel the urgency to know more, this guide—full of relevant science, thoughtful reflections, and practical life lessons—will help you figure it out. *HIT IT OFF* will give you the insight you know is out there but is often unspoken. You should know about this and let it serve as your North Star. Be brave and look to this unique and instructive book. It will significantly advance your work and life. You were just handed a gift. Take it."

—Karnit Braun
Partner, Employee Justice Legal Group

"*HIT IT OFF* is a great playbook for establishing, developing, and furthering relationships of all types. Joe Brocato's 21 Rules are a wonderful compendium to the reader who is looking for personal and professional enrichment through his or her relationship with others. Joe presents each Rule with scientific research to further underscore the efficacy of the 21 Rules. A wonderful motivational book focusing the reader on ways to develop meaningful relationships with others. An absolute must-read."

—Tim Lavender
Partner, National Law Firm

hit it off

21 RULES FOR MASTERING THE ART AND SCIENCE OF RELATIONSHIPS IN LIFE AND BUSINESS

JOE BROCATO

IMAGINE™ & WONDER Publishers, New York

HIT IT OFF: 21 Rules for Mastering the Art and Science of Relationships in Life and Business

Published by Imagine and Wonder Publishers New York
www.ImagineAndWonder.com
Your guarantee of quality

As publishers, we strive to produce every book to the highest commercial standards. The printing and binding have been planned to ensure a sturdy, attractive publication that should give years of enjoyment. If your copy fails to meet our high standards, please inform us and we will gladly replace it. admin@ imagineandwonder.com

ISBN: 9781637610251 (Hardcover)
ISBN: 9781637611029 (Paperback)
ISBN: 9781637611036 (Ebook)
ISBN: 9781637611043 (Audiobook)
Library of Congress Control Number: 2022952079

First Edition
Printed in the USA

Scan this QR code with your phone camera
for more titles from Imagine and Wonder

Thank You

To the Universe and all the people in it who have impacted my life.

Table of Contents

Introduction

HAVE YOU EVER WONDERED why some people seem to naturally hit it off with others?

Are you impressed with how they're able to transform that positive first impression into a relationship that helps them achieve their goals in life or business?

Would you like to deepen your relationships with the people who are important to you?

If so, *HIT IT OFF: 21 Rules for Mastering the Art and Science of Relationships in Life and Business* will be a refreshing and rewarding resource for you.

I often think of two people in my life who embodied these rules and probably didn't even know it. The first was my maternal grandfather. I would be amazed at how he could meet someone and, within just a few minutes, you'd think they were long-time friends. He was smart and humble, and people loved him. The other person was my father, who passed away at a fairly young age. A teenage immigrant from Sicily, he rose to become an alderman in my hometown and was beloved not only by the people he represented, but everyone he met. One might have considered him a simple man with a natural talent to appeal to others. I just considered him my dad.

What these great men and many other people have taught me is that hitting if off with people begins with a basic understanding: Others will only be attracted to us (and stay with us) if we have a certain type of relationship with them.

A great relationship is important, but the *uniqueness* of a relationship matters even more. You want to have unique relationships with people—those that are difficult, if not impossible, to replace. That type of relationship sets you apart from others. It establishes a foundation on which to build a relationship both people want to preserve and grow, since it would be difficult to find that type of bond with someone else. Uniqueness should be the goal of every single one of our relationships because it helps us to maximize the likelihood of our personal and business success and happiness.

How do we establish a unique relationship with people? The answer is surprisingly simple: We tap into one of the most important basic human needs people have. Those who have mastered the art of relationships realize this simple and sincere strategy.

What does everyone want? We all want a connection with others.[1]

Foster unique relationships with other people by focusing on this common thread that runs throughout human existence. One of our greatest gifts as human beings is the opportunity to socialize with other people and develop rewarding feelings around shared values and trust with them. When we make a unique connection with people, we unwrap this gift and allow it to enrich our lives.

While we all have the basic human need for connection with others, our perceptions of others around us differ because of our different

---

[1] R. F. Baumeister and M. R. Leary, "The Need to Belong: Desire for Interpersonal Attachments as a Fundamental Human Motivation," *Psychological Bulletin* 117, no. 3 (1995): 497-529.

personality types and personal histories. Many people bring confidence, happiness, and joy into their relationships in light of their past experiences. But some people harbor degrees of jealousy, resentment, and fear that make it difficult for them to feel comfortable trusting other people. Some people have had tough childhoods or have been let down a lot in their lives. Others may not have had many positive things happen to them and are not very hopeful about their lives. They may not look forward to tomorrow as much as you do. And while many people have impressive skills to perform their jobs, or fancy educations, they don't have basic skills to socialize with other people in a meaningful way—in a way that leads to amazing relationships. The rules in this book will help you break through these sorts of relationship barriers that some people you encounter may have and will encourage you to promote feelings of trust and shared values with them that lead to deeper—more unique—relationships.

Our objective in building relationships should be to focus on everyone's need for human connection. If we do that, we can establish truly unique and long-lasting relationships with people. And when that happens, we have a much better chance of achieving *our* goals in life, whether they be personal or business. Many people do not encounter others who focus on or understand the importance and power of the ideas in this book—which translate into the relative uniqueness of mindfully using these ideas to nurture relationships.

The *21 Rules* are easy to use. They may even appear self-evident. But their simplicity can cause us to ignore them or not focus on them enough in our relationships. Consider the *21 Rules* as tools in your toolbox. Use each tool for the task immediately at hand, as appropriate depending on the situation. You can also think of them as instruments that you practice as you refine your skills. Great musicians practice their instruments regularly. They always get better.

You can use these rules in your everyday life to hit it off with people from the moment you meet them. They'll allow you to make a refreshing and positive first impression. They'll give you the confidence to walk into a new situation with anyone and fit right in, establish rapport, and be perceived as nice and fun, and a person of integrity—someone who can be trusted with business and friendship. You can also use these rules as you continue to get to know people, cultivating unique relationships for a lifetime.

The *21 Rules* are backed up by scientific research that gives you a deeper perspective on their practical usefulness and importance in building relationships. Understanding what science says about these rules also will remind you of the many benefits you will *not* enjoy if you don't practice the rules every day as you establish and grow your relationships. The importance of each rule is further illustrated in this book through real-life "train wreck" stories about what happens when the rules "derail." The good news is that no matter what has happened in the past, you can improve. Stories about the "Zen" of each rule in these pages (many of which touch on personal and sometimes very sensitive experiences in my life) will, I hope, inspire you to envision the many unique relationships that await you in your future. I hope these stories inspire and encourage you to get the most out of each rule.

There is no one way to use these rules. We all have different styles. Some of us are introverts and some are extroverts. Some are in between. It doesn't matter. They work for everyone because they're simple. They are rooted in our fundamental human nature and based on our universal need as human beings to connect with others.

Use these rules every day. Practice them and discover what works for you. Experiment. Start by working through the exercises in this book. Enjoy the reward of building the very best—unique—relationships with other people, those based on shared values and trust. Create win-win relationships and become a master of the art and science of relationships in life and business!

Rule 1

Take a Fresh Look at Eye Contact to Convey Emotion

Where words are restrained, the eyes often talk a great deal.
—Samuel Richardson (English writer)

DO THIS!

Establish and maintain an appropriate level of eye contact during your conversations with others.

WHY?

Scientific studies demonstrate the power of eye contact.

A recent study concludes that "eye contact is a key element that connects humans during social communication."[1] The study found that eye contact primes the social brain to empathize. Empathy—the ability to put yourself in someone else's shoes—builds rapport which helps establish interpersonal connectivity.[2]

---

[1] Takahiko Koike, et al., "What Makes Eye Contact Special? Neural Substrates of On-line Mutual Eye-gaze: A Hyperscanning fMRI Study," *eNeuro* 10 (2019): 1523.

[2] Allison Abbe and Susan E. Brandon, "Building and Maintaining Rapport in Investigative Interviews," *Police Practice and Research* 15, no. 3 (2014): 207-220.

When you meet someone's eyes with yours, you tap into the essence of non-verbal communication. In fact, David Keatley, Director of Researchers in Behaviour Sequence Analysis (ReBSA) at the University of Lincoln, UK, puts it this way: "Eye contact can tell us if someone is listening and attending to us. It can tell us we have their attention. It can then show their emotion—concern, enjoyment, happiness, love."[3]

If you think about it, eye contact is typically the first means of "connection" generally with someone (the reason it is Rule 1). We are immediately drawn to the eyes in any social setting. It is important to take advantage of this automatic human reflex and use eye contact to instantly harness a human connection with someone.

Make eye contact and convey the emotion you have for the other person. In your personal life, eye contact is an efficient and effective way to convey the sincerity of your friendship, your empathy, and your love for the other person. In business, eye contact will help you convey your dedicated attention to a person's business needs and goals. It demonstrates that you are listening to the important aspects of his or her business.

A FEW TIPS ABOUT RULE 1

As your sensitivity to the importance of eye contact evolves, keep these tips in mind:

- Always be socially appropriate when maintaining eye contact. Be mindful not to maintain too much eye contact. No one

---

[3] Nicola Heath, "How Eye-to-Eye Contact Can Help to Heal Your Relationships," https://www.sbs.com.au/topics/voices/relationships/article/2017/08/14/how-eye -eye-contact-can-help-heal-your-relationships.

wants to be stared at in a social or business setting. Let's leave the staring to our pets when they're trying to figure out what we're saying to them!

- The power of eye contact is much less effective if other aspects of communication are distracting. Are you speaking too loudly or softly, too fast or slow? Slumping in your chair or standing too close? Remember that eye contact alone isn't sufficient to develop relationships.

- You benefit if people recognize your empathy for them through your eyes. Convey your empathy for someone by listening to and learning about that person.

- Combine a smile (Rule 3) with eye contact when appropriate. This is really important at the beginning of a conversation with someone you just met. Convey your joy and excitement about the interaction with the other person by sharing a genuine smile.

- Remember that our eyes can reveal ourselves and our mood to others, whether we intend to do this or not. People can tell from our eyes in many cases if we are happy or sad, excited or fearful, etc. Our eyes convey our inner person and are powerful parts of our personhood.

TRAIN WRECK: WHEN RULE 1 DERAILS

The appropriate use of eye contact can be almost non-detectable because it's typically natural and expected. Unfortunately, the inappropriate use of eye contact—especially the lack of eye contact—is terribly noticeable and could derail trust in a relationship. Given my role as an attorney and businessperson, I am in different social settings every day. At a business development get-together recently, one of the participants was more interested in the game on TV than in our conversation. Whenever he spoke, he stared at the TV and expected the rest of us to pay attention to him. Once in a while, he would look at the others, but only for a second, before returning to the game. I had never met the person before and regrettably the only lasting emotion I have for that person isn't positive. The only good news is that, after a while, I followed his lead and watched the game as he spoke (why not?), and my team won!

THE ZEN OF RULE 1

Putting aside the science for a second, just think back to when you decided to pursue a romantic relationship or go into business with someone. Was there something about that person's eyes that gave you the trust to move forward? My guess: there was. Next time you meet someone, pay close attention to the eyes. Some say that they are windows to a person's soul. They help us reveal ourselves to others. And they allow people into our minds and hearts—into our soul. Start to notice how someone's eyes reflect their emotional state, whether happy or sad, excited or worried, or any number of other emotions. As people reveal themselves to you through their eyes, be thankful for the gift they are giving you. Give a similar gift back to them by using your eyes to reveal yourself and allow them in. Do so and create an experience that is rewarding for everyone.

KEY TAKEAWAY

Use eye contact to establish a sincere connection with others and hit it off.

Rule 2

Prepare to Achieve Goals Efficiently—In Reverse

In preparing for battle I have always found that plans are useless, but planning is indispensable.

—Dwight D. Eisenhower (34th U.S. President)

DO THIS!

Set reasonable goals—in reverse—to fully develop a relationship.

WHY?

Whether after a first encounter with someone or during the later development of a relationship, you need to have a plan to develop that relationship. Leaving the development of any relationship to chance is planning to fail. But research shows that the best way to plan and set goals is to do so in reverse. It sounds counterintuitive but makes sense. Researchers at Korea Business School and the University of Iowa found that people are more likely to achieve their goals when they engage in something called "future retrospection."[1]

---

[1] Jooyoung Park, et al., "Relative Effects of Forward and Backward Planning on Goal Pursuit," *Psychological Science* 28, no. 11 (2017): 1620-1630, doi:10.1177/0956797617715510.

Basically, we imagine ourselves as if we've already accomplished our goal, and we then plan backwards, thinking about all the steps that we had to take to get to that goal.[2] The researchers found that this increases our productivity, motivation, and confidence, and reduces stress as we pursue our goal.[3] When we plan forward, there seem to be endless pathways to the particular goal that can end up confusing us as to where we should start now, and our goal seems far into the future, which can reduce our motivation to proceed.[4]

In the context of developing a relationship, start with imagining that you and the other person have a certain type of close relationship, in your personal life or in business, whatever the situation is. Clearly envision that as your goal. Now work backwards and think about how you felt when you finally had that type of relationship with that person. Did you celebrate? Now ask yourself: What did you do to develop the relationship a week before you reached that goal? One month before? Three months before? Six months before? How about a year before? Then think about what you did this week. What did you do today? And THAT is where you start right now—today. By going through this exercise, you're likely to have much greater clarity around how to move forward to develop the relationship.

A FEW TIPS ABOUT RULE 2

- Write down your end goal for a relationship. In your personal life, if you meet someone you could imagine marrying some-day, you might write down: Be happily married and live in a

---

[2] Id.
[3] Id.
[4] Id.

particular town and type of house. Do the same for business goals.

- Work cooperatively with the other person to set an end goal for the relationship. In business, you might agree with a potential client that, if the relationship develops as you both hope, you might have the opportunity of doing a deal or otherwise working together.

- If you sense the other person isn't on board for where you'd like to see the relationship go, then redirect your energy to another person who has a similar goal, or simply modify the initial goal to one that will still be rewarding to you.

- As you think backwards about the things you have done to lead toward a goal, consider the details. For example, when thinking about an important dinner with someone, determine the restaurant, other guests, something to do after dinner, etc.

- After you finish thinking in reverse, remember that your plan is a good start, not a finished product. Something may happen as you start working with the plan that may render steps in the future irrelevant or less effective. Don't be afraid to make changes.

TRAIN WRECK: WHEN RULE 2 DERAILS

This one is super personal. Weight loss—or lack of it. Mine. In my never-ending quest to reach my ideal body weight, normal goal planning for me had been a disaster for years. I'd always start with a diet and workout schedule that seemed to make sense, then proceed to getting in a routine after a couple of months, followed by some weight loss after several months, with the hope of achieving my end goal of a decent amount of weight loss after, say, a year. Guess what? Failure—major derailment—every time! Until . . . I planned in reverse. Planning in reverse meant envisioning a year from then being at my ideal weight with a mindset to eat healthy and have a workout routine that can have a chance of lasting a lifetime. Then I worked backwards from there, essentially making good progress after six months, and getting into a routine for working out after one month and starting with a consideration of a number of different approaches to dieting and exercising before selecting any particular one. What this did was cause me to realize that without the right mindset to begin with, the chances of reaching my goal would be fruitless. When I had just planned "forward," I had never truly appreciated the importance of mindset. And planning in reverse gave me the chance to get specific on dates for completion of milestone goals, again, not something I was focused on when planning as I had always done. The good news is that planning in reverse was productive and helped me get much closer to my ideal weight. The bad news (further derailment?): after about a year into my quest, they built a Krispy Kreme doughnuts way too close to my house!

THE ZEN OF RULE 2

As an avid fan of business development, I love to work with people as they think through their business development plan. There are no strict rules when it comes to new customer or client development. Everyone has his or her own style. Whatever works, works. That's really the bottom line. But having some sense of structure before you start is always smart. When I work with people who do not have much experience developing business, it is understandable to start thinking about things you can do right now when you start and *then* to envision your future success after doing all these cool things over the next days, weeks, and months. Before I had fully considered the concept of "future retrospection" discussed in this Rule 2, I had mapped out a business development plan outline for people to use if they wanted. Vision comes first (end goal), long-term objectives (way into the future) next, then short-term goals (a shorter time in the future), and finally immediate action items (what to do at the start—right now). Think about business development (or anything else in life) that way—with the end in mind—and work backwards. By doing this, you free your mind from the minute details of the specifics, and you can focus on the broader picture, while backing into those details creatively as you think through the overall plan and achieve your end goal. When I work with people on goal setting, I love seeing the light bulb go off as they work through the reverse planning process. It's fun to watch—that's my reward.

KEY TAKEAWAY

Plan for goal development, but plan in reverse.

Rule 3

Remember That a Simple Smile Is Tied to Deep Trust

A smile is the light in your window that tells others that there is a caring, sharing person inside.

—Denis Waitley (American motivational speaker)

DO THIS!

Smile when you greet someone, and use your smile to show your enthusiasm and happiness during a conversation.

WHY?

A prominent study found that a genuine smile can really help you strike up a new relationship with someone.[1] The researchers determined that people are much more receptive to positive emotions when forming new bonds than they are to negative emotions. This is powerful because the study also found that humans tune into the

---

[1] Belinda Campos, Dominik Schoebi, Gian C. Gonzaga, Shelly L. Gable, and Dacher Keltner. "Attuned to the Positive? Awareness and Responsiveness to Others' Positive Emotion Experience and Display," *Motivation and Emotion* (2015), DOI: 10.1007/s11031-015-9494-x.

positive almost instinctively. Instinct is tied to our fundamental essence as human beings, similar to how we all have a desire for human connectivity.

If we smile when we first meet someone, we draw out of the other person an instinctual, positive response—the desired response we want because it brings us closer to the other person and vice versa. During a conversation, if you feel enthused about what you are talking about, smile. If you are happy during a conversation, show your happiness with an appropriate smile—you are likely to elicit one in return. One Swedish study suggests that we are likely to react with a smile of our own when someone smiles at us, creating a pleasant and relationship-building loop of happiness.[2]

Science also shows that smiling is tied to trust. In one study, increased smile intensity was associated with greater trustworthiness.[3] Since trust is important in any relationship, using genuine smiles to help build trust with other people is an invaluable asset in mastering the art and science of relationships, especially unique ones.

A FEW TIPS ABOUT RULE 3

- Smiling appropriately means smiling just enough—not too little and not too much. Smiling too much, for example, can lead someone to believe you aren't serious about the

[2] U. Dimberg and S. Söderkvist, "The Voluntary Facial Action Technique: A Method to Test the Facial Feedback Hypothesis," *J Nonverbal Behav* 35 (2011): 17–33, https://doi.org/10.1007/s10919-010-0098-6.

[3] K. Schmidt, R. Levenstein, and Z. Ambadar, "Intensity of Smiling and Attractiveness as Facial Signals of Trustworthiness in Women," *Percept Mot Skills* 114, no. 3 (June 2012): 964-78, doi: 10.2466/07.09.21.PMS.114.3.964-978. PMID: 22913033.

REMEMBER THAT A SIMPLE SMILE IS TIED TO DEEP TRUST | 33

relationship or, worse yet, that you're a buffoon. Leave buffoo-nery to clowns in the circus!

- Only smile if it's genuine. Most people can read a fake smile. An insincere smile is hard to undo. Once someone believes you're fake, then any chance of trust is gone and the hope of continuing the relationship with that person is likely low or non-existent.

- Tie your smile to good eye contact (Rule 1). Eye contact is key to relationship-building. Combine a genuine smile with a tactful look in the eye and double the chances of getting the response you want from the other person.

- When someone smiles at you, smile back if appropriate. Just as you're hoping to show enthusiasm and happiness with your smile, so is the other person. If someone is trying to elicit a responsive smile from you, not smiling back can come off as disrespectful.

- Even if a full-on smile isn't appropriate, using your facial features to show positivity can be helpful in building a rela-tionship. For example, keeping the sides of your mouth pit-ched slightly upward and gently nodding as the other person is speaking will demonstrate a sense of interest and engagement.

TRAIN WRECK: WHEN RULE 3 DERAILS

No Jokers, please! Fans of Batman surely have the image of the Joker's permanent smile etched in their minds—a distinctive fea-ture of the personality (or lack of one) behind the character. If you frequently socialize, you have likely encountered Jokers—typically, people who find it necessary to smile at all times while they speak. The less-than-sincere permanence to their smile becomes distracting. At a conference once, I met someone who was otherwise friendly, but had the Joker smile. We chatted for a few minutes, and not once did he rest his face. I started to wonder if I had said something funny, but I hadn't. I almost wanted to crack a joke to make myself feel more comfortable as we talked, but I didn't. He focused his eyes appropriately on me as he spoke, but the smile was always wide, even when he spoke seriously about the topic of our conversation. As he spoke, all I could think about was getting back home to watch some old Batman episodes from the original TV show. It had been many years since I watched the original series. Although the Joker smile was distracting, I credit that person for getting me back into watching one of my favorite childhood TV series. That said, skip the Joker smile!

THE ZEN OF RULE 3

One of my favorite things to do is to get people to smile. Life can be difficult. Sometimes it seems like there are endless roadblocks to our happiness. Any break from the fight to live happily is welcomed. If I get a sense that someone is stressed out or having a bad day or worried about something, I enjoy trying to lighten their load by simply smiling when I say hi. It's so easy to do. It shouts: It'll be OK. It may not make all the difference in the world to someone, but I think it means something. I notice how people sometimes don't smile at others entering an elevator when they are looking right at each other. Or at the person checking them out in a store. Or at their server in a restaurant. I could never quite understand that. That first encounter is priceless. Even though brief, a smile can pick someone up and give them a feeling of hope that there are decent people out there. If we give nothing else to each other, let's share a smile together when we can.

KEY TAKEAWAY

Your smile is an important relationship-building tool and can help you hit it off with people if you share it with others genuinely and appropriately.

Rule 4

Consciously Listen to Build Acceptance

One of the most sincere forms of respect is actually listening to what another has to say.

—Bryant H. McGill (American activist)

DO THIS!

Make a sincere effort to hear someone's true message, not just the words that person is using.

WHY?

Listening is not a passive act. It is not just about receiving or hearing. It's the "conscious processing of the auditory stimuli that have been perceived through hearing."[1] We need to *consciously* listen to the other person during a conversation so we can hear the complete message of that individual—this is active listening. It takes some effort, but by listening actively, we increase our chances of

---

[1] R. West and L. H. Turner, *Understanding Interpersonal Communication*, 2nd ed. (Boston, USA: Cengage Learning, 2010).

connecting with that individual in a unique way. Connection is more likely because, through active listening, we "demonstrate unconditional acceptance and unbiased reflection."[2] If someone does not feel accepted, it is unlikely that individual will open up and be willing to connect with us.

When we listen actively, we give our full attention to someone and show that we are listening by nodding occasionally, smiling when something is said that is intended to bring out a smile, and encouraging the other person to continue speaking with gentle comments like "yes," and "uh-huh." We allow someone to complete a point before asking a question. We don't judge the other person as that individual is speaking based on our own personal biases. We respond to others in a way that we would want to be treated.

By giving our full attention to someone, we maximize the chance of really "hearing" what that person is trying to say. We hear not only the spoken words, but we try to understand the thought process of the other person.[3] When we understand someone's thought process, and that individual is confident that he or she is truly being heard, that person will feel accepted and be more willing to connect with us.

A FEW TIPS ABOUT RULE 4

- To listen actively to someone, you need to stay focused on the other person and what he or she is saying. Avoid thinking about what to say next the entire time someone is speaking.

---

[2] H. Weger, G. R. Castle, and M. C. Emmett, "Active Listening in Peer Interviews: The Influence of Message Paraphrasing on Perceptions of Listening Skill," *International Journal of Listening* 24, no. 1 (2010): 34-49.

[3] O. Ucok, "Transparency, Communication and Mindfulness," *Journal of Management Development* 25, no. 10 (2006): 1024-1028.

Listen without a predetermined goal or outcome in mind. Ignore side conversations around you.

- Once focused on the speaker, think deeply about what that person is saying. Don't settle for a superficial interpretation of the words alone. Put yourself in the speaker's shoes and consider the words used in context with that person's personality, demeanor, tone of voice, and body movements.

- Ask questions to clarify the intent of the other person to demonstrate that you heard what was said and, more importantly, that you're interested in it. This will help assure to the other person that you "got it."

- Summarize someone's comments when appropriate. This gives you the opportunity to confirm your understanding of what was said. Give the speaker comfort that you actually care about what he or she has said.

- Be respectful (Rule 17) when you respond to what the other person said. For example, it would be disrespectful to immediately hammer the other person with strong opinions that are different from those of the speaker or to be insincere—patronizing—in your response.

TRAIN WRECK: WHEN RULE 4 DERAILS

Ever feel like you're always repeating yourself? I was at dinner with friends just days before this writing, and it happened again to me. We had four people, and sitting right across from me was a nice guy who was friends with one of the other guests. Since we were directly across the table, we'd periodically break into conversation, just the two of us. Random topics—frankly, it was a lot of small talk. He had the eye contact and appropriate smile rules nailed, but he must have asked me to repeat what I said at least ten times! Active listening is not only listening to the words but accurately understanding the message. This otherwise great person was simply not even listening to the words. I could tell he was distracted by just about everything around us—the others at the table and their conversation, other patrons, the waiter, the way the table wasn't level on the ground and moving a little as we spoke. Basically, he was paying attention to everything but me and what I was saying. Mind you, I am not the most interesting conversationalist (although I'm sure my mother would take issue with that!), but I wasn't reciting the dictionary in another language either. Stay focused. Listen. Actively.

THE ZEN OF RULE 4

One of the fondest memories I have as a child is listening to the adults in the room. Believe it or not, I didn't talk a lot when I was young. I can hear my friends shouting as they're reading this: "We don't believe it! Now, you never shut up!" Okay, that's true, but back then I really enjoyed listening and learning. I found the adults to be super interesting and, to this day, I'm thankful for keeping my mouth shut. (Believe me, I am making up for it these days!) A number of years later, I realized how much I would have missed if I had been talking instead of listening. Next time you're in a room and have the urge to speak up, try laying low. Let others talk. Instead of piping up, simply listen and soak in everything they're saying. It's actually quite liberating to sit back and observe and be a sponge for the insight of others. Practicing this sort of listening can help give you a deeper perspective on the context around the words people choose to use, all because you are speaking less and listening more.

KEY TAKEAWAY

Listen with the goal of fully understanding what the other person is really trying to say.

Rule 5

Share Personal Experiences to Create Relationship Depth

Talk to someone about themselves and they'll listen for hours.
—Dale Carnegie (American author)

DO THIS!

Learn about people through the mutual sharing of personal life details.

WHY?

Building a meaningful and unique relationship with someone involves a mutual give-and-take with that person.[1] When people share personal details about themselves, such as their feelings, thoughts, and memories, they are more likely to build a deep and trusting relationship.[2]

---

[1] S. Sprecher, S. Treger, J. D. Wondra, N. Hilaire, and K. Wallpe, "Taking Turns: Reciprocal Self-disclosure Promotes Liking in Initial Interactionsm," *Journal of Experimental Social Psychology* 49, no. 5 (September 2013): 860-6, doi:10.1016/j.jesp.2013.03.017.

[2] H. Kreiner and Y. Levi-Belz, "Self-Disclosure Here and Now: Combining Retrospective Perceived Assessment With Dynamic Behavioral Measures," *Front Psychol.* 10 (Mar 28, 2019): 558, doi:10.3389/fpsyg.2019.00558

This process of sharing personal details about ourselves is called self-disclosure.[3]

In both initial and later conversations with someone, sincerely encourage the other person to share some degree of personal information with you. Do this by offering up personal details about *your* life to the extent you feel comfortable doing that. By taking the lead with self-disclosure, the other person will be more comfortable opening up and doing the same thing. The other person may actually feel compelled to share personal information with you. This phenomenon is called the norm of reciprocity when we feel pressure to share with someone who has already shared something about his or her own life and feelings with us.[4] When we share something intimate, we create an imbalance of sorts. The other person all of sudden knows a lot about us, but not the other way around, so that person will feel the need to share something personal about him- or herself.

In practicing mutual self-disclosure, it is important to avoid any information that might be deemed inappropriate by the other person. Be mindful of the stage of the relationship. Oversharing early on in the relationship might make the other individual uncomfortable. Inappropriate or ill-timed self-disclosure could make someone feel embarrassed and cause that person to question your judgement. Gauge the level of disclosure to the degree of intimacy you have created with the other person to ensure that all information disclosed is conveyed and received with the utmost level of appropriateness and respect without resulting in the opposite of what you intend (i.e., a poor or damaged relationship).

---

[3] Id.
[4] Sprecher et al. "Taking Turns," 860-6.

A FEW TIPS ABOUT RULE 5

- Remember this one simple statement when you first meet someone: "Tell me a little bit about yourself." It's the perfect icebreaker, puts the other person at ease, and gives him or her the opportunity to take control of the conversation for a while.

- Think about beginning mutual self-disclosure by sharing information about your family. This can be a great way to get the other person to talk about his or her family, a comfortable topic for many people.

- Share a personal detail about yourself that few people know. This is a big step in showing someone how you feel comfortable with them. But never share a detail about yourself unless you are 100% comfortable doing so.

- Ask open-ended questions earlier in the relationship. This makes people feel most comfortable as you get to know them. Use more direct questions about the person after getting to know him or her more. Once people feel more comfortable with you, they will be more willing to share specific personal information.

- If someone shares something that is difficult for that person to say (i.e., how they made a mistake), then consider sharing something similar. This will put the person in a more comfortable position about having told you, and he or she will consider you a closer friend for it.

TRAIN WRECK: WHEN RULE 5 DERAILS

Ever get caught on the wrong side of a bell curve? I oftentimes think of life as a bell curve. Most of us are in the middle, with extremes on either side. In conversations with new people, most people are equally interested in learning about the other person. Then, on one end of the bell curve, there are those who prod and poke, eliciting details of your life out of you and never share anything about themselves; on the other end, there are those who literally couldn't care less about you and your story. I was out of town with a buddy of mine a couple of months ago and got together with a newer acquaintance of mine who was living down there. I wanted to get to know him better. We grabbed lunch, and I swear that I listened to him talk for more than an hour and a half before he asked me one question about myself. Don't get me wrong: he's an interesting guy. But he was completely self-absorbed and, quite frankly, I don't think he even realized it. As he droned on, I longed to be in the middle of the bell curve, not so much because I have so many interesting things to say (actually, I have very few interesting things to say—except for the *21 Rules* in this book, of course!), but the one-sided nature of the personal disclosure process was sadly limiting our ability to connect.

THE ZEN OF RULE 5

One of the greatest honors of my life was to work for a titan in the legal industry right out of law school. His name was Peer Pedersen. Peer had a keen intellect and was a brave entrepreneur. Before his death a number of years ago, I had begun writing his biography. I just felt that a book about his fascinating life journey needed to be written. Every week we would meet in his office, and I would ask him questions about his life, his career, his hopes and dreams, and just about everything else I could think to ask him. Quite regrettably, Peer passed away before we completed much of the interview process, and I never wrote his biography—I still needed too much personal perspective on his life to do the biography justice. But the gift he gave me was the connection we formed throughout that process. Thinking back, I honestly feel that he disclosed to me personal information he had never disclosed to anyone else. We went from professional colleagues to something much greater than that. He trusted me with sensitive information. During our time together, I, too, shared personal information with him. The process brought us closer together. If there is someone in your life you admire, sit down with that person and share something personal. Hopefully that person will share something in return. It is quite a powerful feeling.

KEY TAKEAWAY

The more you learn about someone and the more he or she learns about you, the more unique the relationship.

Rule 6

Build Connection Through Trust

*Everybody is going to have their own issues that they bring
to the table, but for me, the best thing is just giving over
to whatever is there and trusting whatever is there and enjoying it.*

—Johnny Simmons (American actor)

DO THIS!

Trust people within reason because trust is critical to building unique, long-term relationships.

WHY?

Trust is pretty much everything. Global authority on trust Stephen M. R. Covey suggests that "the way we solve problems and get things done is with and through people. And nothing is more impactful on people, their work, and their performance than trust."[1] The entire idea of forming a relationship with people is to get something done, whether to feel happier, safer, more productive, more successful, etc. Building mutual trust with others then becomes an important

---

[1] "Ten Reasons Why," https://www.speedoftrust.com/.

relationship-building skill. Relationship expert John Gottman concludes that "trust is essential to healthy relationships."[2] Since trust between two people is critical to relationship development, without it there can be no truly meaningful connection between them.

An unfortunate reality is that "in many communities and organizations throughout the world, there is a growing trust deficit."[3] As much as we would like to think people are willing to simply trust us, many people are rightfully cautious about where they place their trust. But the growing trust deficit is an advantage for those of us who engender sincere trust and are, in fact, trustworthy. By focusing on the importance of trust in relationships, especially in light of such a trust deficit, we can increase the possibility of fostering relationships with others founded on mutual trust.

As you think about trust in the context of relationship building, keep in mind that it is essentially a confident belief in the reliability, truth, and ability or strength of someone or something.[4] If another person is to trust you, he or she must have that firm belief in you. You must approach the relationship from the very start and during that relationship with an eye toward fostering belief in you. That way, you maximize the likelihood of the other person beginning to trust you. When trust is perceived by that person, the relationship matures and both people become more connected.

---

[2] https://greatergood.berkeley.edu/article/item/john_gottman_on_trust_and _betrayal.

[3] Andrew T. Soderberg and Alexander C. Romney, "Building Trust: How Leaders Can Engender Feelings of Trust Among Followers," *Business Horizons* (2021): ISSN 0007-6813, https://doi.org/10.1016/j.bushor.2021.02.031.

[4] S. Marsh, M. Dibben, P. Herrmann, V. Issarny and S. Shiu, "Trust, Untrust, Distrust and Mistrust—An Exploration of the Dark(er) Side," *Trust Management* 3477 (Berlin and Heidelberg: Springer, 2005):17–33.

Building trust can be done in different ways with different people. Here are just a few research-backed ways to build trust. First, align values with the other person and communicate about them often.[5] Try emphasizing how much you value respecting others, or the mission around your organization, or the importance of honesty in all that you do. These are common values that foster connection with others. Be humble in your interactions with others; humility goes a long way to being perceived as trustworthy by others.[6] And being compassionate with other people is also a great way to encourage trust.[7]

A FEW TIPS ABOUT RULE 6

- Have a good reason to trust others. Make sure the other person's values align with yours. Make sure they, too, are humble and compassionate. Without such basic qualities, trusting someone else can be riskier than normal.

- During your conversations, tell stories about how you've proven your trust to others in the past. Explain how people have trusted you and you've come through for them. Let people know you have a track record for being honest and trustworthy.

- Pay attention to someone's experiences of having been let down in the past, and then steer clear of any way that person

[5] R. Mayer, J. Davis and F. Schoorman, "An Integrative Model of Organizational Trust." *The Academy of Management Review* 20, no. 3 (1995): 709-734. doi:10 .2307/258792.

[6] Andrew T. Soderberg and Alexander C. Romney, "Building Trust: How Leaders Can Engender Feelings of Trust Among Followers," *Business Horizons*, (2021), ISSN 0007-6813, https://doi.org/10.1016/j.bushor.2021.02.031.

[7] Id.

might feel you're doing the same thing in your relationship. Sometimes people have different interpretations of what it means to be let down.

- Share details about when you were let down by someone and how that affected you and how you'd never want someone to feel the same way. Everyone has been let down, and acknowledging your sensitivity to the concept of trust based on your prior experiences can bring people closer together.

- If you do unintentionally let someone down, immediately admit your mistake (Rule 11) and sincerely promise to never let that person down again. We all make mistakes. We're far from perfect. People will forgive most mistakes if given a heartfelt apology.

TRAIN WRECK: WHEN RULE 6 DERAILS

Now you see it, now you don't! When someone enters your life who appears to be a promising new friend, you tend to see all the benefits of friendship and are comforted by the rug of potential camaraderie—we want to see people as they portray themselves to us. But when the rug is pulled out from under us, the promise of camaraderie disappears. A number of years ago, a good friend of mine introduced me to one of her guy friends when we were all out in the same group. The guy and I hit it off and, as it turned out, we liked the same type of music. As a big-time music fan, I immediately saw him as a potential buddy. We bonded and became good friends for nearly a year. Unfortunately, as events unraveled, it turned out he was a complete fraud. He had no fewer than fifteen alias names, was being sued for numerous shady reasons by many people, and was scamming everyone around him for whatever he could get. Once the veil had been lifted, I realized that the trust I had put in him as a friend was misplaced. He was not the person I thought he was. Needless to say, we immediately parted ways. Unfortunately, this happens to a lot of people a lot of the time. My situation is not special. But it reinforced the importance of trust in cementing a relationship and the damage the absence of trust can inflict on an otherwise great connection between people. Just my luck: couldn't he have been from Publishers Clearing House coming into my life to award me a multi-million-dollar prize?

THE ZEN OF RULE 6

"Fool me once, shame on you. Fool me twice, shame on me." We all know the saying. And it's true. No one wants to be taken advantage of. Once we are burned by someone, we tend to be very fearful of trusting others in similar situations, whether in the context of friendship (including a romantic one) or business. But living in fear ties us down and takes away the potential of living life to the fullest. I had a terrible experience many years ago when I trusted the founders of a company with a lot of money. I had really hoped my investment would work out, and instead it was a bust, all because the founders of the company were not the best people. For a long time, I had a hard time trusting people who wanted me to invest with them. But one day it occurred to me that if I never invested in another deal again, I would never realize a big return. Sitting on the sidelines seemed more frustrating than having lost money. Eventually, I started investing again and trusting good people to put my money to good use. Luckily, things have worked out well (so far!). Breaking through the fear and opening myself up to potential loss for a greater good felt amazing and still does. Be fearless sometimes. Live with trust as much as you can. There are way more good people in the world that bad, and it's an awesome feeling to trust other people when it makes sense to do so.

KEY TAKEAWAY

Relationships are built on trust, so work intentionally to build trust with others.

Rule 7

Provide Value to Promote Gratitude

Strive not to be a success, but rather to be of value.
—Albert Einstein (Theoretical physicist)

DO THIS!

Build a network of valuable friends, and figure out how you can help other people with those contacts.

WHY?

Providing some sort of value to people strengthens relationships and contributes to relationship connection and satisfaction.[1] Adam Grant, author of *Give & Take,* believes it is important to be "otherish"—the willingness to give more than you receive—but still keep your own interests in sight.[2] By providing value to someone, you

---

[1] A. Wood, J. Froh, and A. Geraghty, "Gratitude and Well-being: A Review and Theoretical Integration." *Clinical Psychology Review* 30 (2010): 890-905. doi:10 .1016/j.cpr.2010.03.005.

[2] Adam M. Grant, *Give and Take: A Revolutionary Approach to Success,* (New York, NY: Viking, 2013).

will promote feelings of gratitude in that person. We are all likely to feel grateful if we think we have a positive personal outcome that we have not earned or are otherwise not deserving of—due to the actions of someone else.[3]

When people feel gratitude toward us, they will look for ways to return the favor based on their appreciation for what we have done for them. The experience of gratitude inspires others who have benefited from acts of kindness to repay their benefactors.[4] When someone returns a favor, especially in a way that helps you, you benefit and are closer to achieving your goals in life or business.

There are makers and takers in the world. You want to be a maker, someone who creates and provides value to others. Takers simply take from others, in many cases without showing appreciation. Takers are like parasites on a host. They suck people dry. You want to be the exact opposite and be perceived by others as a maker. Be giving and generous, and leverage the relationships you have with other people to, in turn, provide value to the people who are important in your life. By doing that, others will be drawn to you.

A FEW TIPS ABOUT RULE 7

- Make an inventory of the value you can provide to people. Examples might include providing access to needed

---

[3] R. A. Emmons and M.E. McCullough, "Counting Blessings Versus Burdens: An Experimental Investigation of Gratitude and Subjective Well-being in Daily Life," *Journal of Personality and Social Psychology* 84, no. 2 (2003): 377.

[4] M. E. McCullough, M. B. Kimeldorf and A. D. Cohen, "An Adaptation for Altruism: The Social Causes, Social Effects, and Social Evolution of Gratitude," *Current Directions in Psychological Science* 17, no. 4 (2008): 281-285, doi:10 .1111/j.1467-8721.2008.00590.x.

information or a business connection, making an introduction to someone they've wanted to meet, being a trusted friend and someone to do things with, etc.

- Ask people how you can help them. Let others know you just want to be helpful and a good partner to help them achieve their goals in life and business. Once you have a good idea of what people want or need, you can be more efficient in delivering value to them.

- Be creative as you think about providing value. For example, if you and the other person share a passion for helping promote arts in education, brainstorm ways you can collaborate and maybe start an organization to raise money for this cause.

- Always be growing your value network. If you are in business, keep expanding your network of contacts with excellent people in different industries so you can build a broad reach of friends across the business world. In life, generally, continue to meet new and interesting people who are in positions of influence.

- When you ask someone for a favor to help another person, make sure you are deeply appreciative and return the favor. You don't want to provide value to one person and damage a relationship with another by being perceived as a user.

TRAIN WRECK: WHEN RULE 7 DERAILS

Once I was introduced by a close friend to his wealth manager. When the guy called me, I mentioned that I already have a trusted financial advisor but would certainly take a meeting with him to network.

When I arrived at the Starbucks, he reached into his briefcase and pulled out a formal wealth management presentation for me. He had clearly not been practicing active listening (Rule 4) during our phone conversation! He insisted on going through the motions as I sipped my coffee. After he was done, he reached back into his briefcase and pulled out a half-inch of contact pages from my LinkedIn profile. He said, "I meet with five people a day, and get eight leads from each of them. I'd like to walk you through some of your LinkedIn contacts and have you introduce me to them." Good thing I had already finished my coffee, because I'd have likely choked on it as he was spewing this disrespectful garbage. He was a user. A taker. Not a giver or a maker. All he wanted was something from me. He had zero interest in helping me or simply being professional. Given my respect for my friend who had introduced us, I recommended that he call me in a month to grab lunch and get to know each other first before I opened up my vast network of contacts to him. Guess what? Never heard from this character ever again. And that's a good thing, although I'm still curious as to which introductions he wanted!

THE ZEN OF RULE 7

I've been truly blessed to have friends all over the world in different lines of work. When working with people in business, I enjoy using my network to help them accomplish their goals, like making a strategic introduction to someone else I know. But as much as I enjoy providing value to others in business, when it comes to using my relationships to help family and close friends, there's no comparison. Most recently, my three teenage sons expressed an interest in learning about the stock market. They wanted to start investing some of their modest savings. I wish I had had their entrepreneurial spirit when I was their age! They soaked up as much information as they could online and asked me some questions. Although I am no stock expert, I know many professionals who are experts. I offered to reach out to a few of them and ask them to speak with my boys, giving them a crash course by phone on picking stocks. I was honored that the friends I asked to help said yes immediately. We got on the phone with them and they educated my sons on their personal approach to picking stocks. Fast forward months later, all of my kids are invested in the market with some of the very best advice from top financial experts. Nothing feels as good as helping family and close friends with the contacts you have. Enjoy that feeling. Embrace it. Practice using your network of friends to help those you love and care for.

KEY TAKEAWAY

Be valuable to people, and they will reward you with respect and sincere friendship.

Rule 8

Use Humor to Convey a Similar Worldview

Humor is mankind's greatest blessing.
—Mark Twain (American writer)

DO THIS!

Weave tasteful humor into your conversations.

WHY?

Shared laughter is tied to relationship satisfaction according to social science research.[1] It can communicate to others that we have a similar worldview, which strengthens our relationships.[2] Social psychologist, Sara Algoe, has stated that "[f]or people who are laughing together, shared laughter signals that they see the world in

---

[1] L. E. Kurtz and S. B. Algoe, "Putting Laughter in Context: Shared Laughter as Behavioral Indicator of Relationship Well-being." *Personal Relationships*, 22 (2015): 573-590.

[2] L. E. Kurtz and S. B. Algoe, "When Sharing a Laugh Means Sharing More: Testing the Role of Shared Laughter on Short-Term Interpersonal Consequences," *J Nonverbal Behav* 41 (2017): 45–65, https://doi.org/10.1007/s10919-016-0245-9.

the same way, and it momentarily boosts their sense of connection. Perceived similarity ends up being an important part of the story of relationships."[3]

Humor is tied to attractiveness in romantic relationships.[4] In fact, a good sense of humor is one of the most sought out characteristics in a romantic partner.[5] And in business, the appropriate use of humor can make us more motivating and admired by others.[6] Behavioral scientist Jennifer Aaker and media and strategy consultant Naomi Bagdonas recognize how aspiring executives and entrepreneurs can leverage laughter for better relationships and business results.[7] No matter the type of relationship, humor connects us and fosters relationships.

Success generally in the workplace is dependent on developing excellent relationships with leadership, coworkers, and employees. Michael Kerr, an international business speaker, president of *Humor at Work*, and author of *The Humor Advantage: Why Some Businesses Are Laughing All the Way to the Bank*, has stated that "humor is a fabulous icebreaker and can tear down walls, can help people build relationships in the workplace, and especially these days,

---

[3] https://greatergood.berkeley.edu/article/item/how_laughter_brings_us_together.

[4] Jeffrey Hall, "Sexual Selection and Humor in Courtship: A Case for Warmth and Extroversion," *Evolutionary Psychology* 13 (2015), 10.1177/1474704915598918.

[5] E. R. Bressler, R. A. Martin and S. Balshine, "Production and Appreciation of Humor as Sexually Selected Trait," *Evolution and Human Behavior* 27 (2006): 121–130. doi:10.1016/j.evolhumbehav.2005.09.001.

[6] W. H. Decker, "Managerial Humor and Subordinate Satisfaction," *Social Behavior and Personality: An International Journal* 15, no. 2 (1987): 225-232.

[7] Jennifer Aaker and Naomi Bagdonas, *Humor, Seriously: Why Humor Is a Secret Weapon in Business and Life (And How Anyone Can Harness It. Even You)*, (Currency: Illustrated edition, February 2, 2021).

relationships are critical to success."[8] Weaving humor tastefully into your conversations with people can increase your personal and business success.

A FEW TIPS ABOUT RULE 8

- Make sure your humor is tasteful. Inappropriate humor is a sure way to end a relationship. Although people might initially laugh, when the dust settles, the other person will question your judgment and integrity.
- Rule 8 is not a suggestion to become a professional comedian. If you happen to be one, then by all means use your skills to create an environment where the other person is in a good mood and entertained. But if you aren't, don't start telling canned jokes or pretending to be someone you're not.
- Think about funny things in your life. For example, if your dog likes to carry its own leash on a walk, and the other person tells you a story about his or her dog doing something cute, then share the story about your leash-toting canine.
- Look for cues to be humorous. Spontaneity is much better than canned jokes. For example, as people speak, use your active listening skills (Rule 4) and be attentive to creative ways of telling a funny story or making a humorous comment that is appropriate.
- Respond to someone's humor appropriately. Laughing too much will be considered condescending. But smiling and

[8] Michael Kerr, *10 Reasons Why Humour Is A Key To Success At Work*, https://www.kmprod.com/blog/michael-kerr-humor-in-the-workplace-motivator/.

laughing, just enough, is a form of acceptance and when someone feels accepted, he or she will feel more connected with you.

TRAIN WRECK: WHEN RULE 8 DERAILS

"I'm funny how? I mean funny like I'm a clown? I amuse you?" Remember that iconic scene from the movie Goodfellas, when Tommy is getting confrontational with his friend Henry over something funny Tommy had said? There's nothing like a good laugh, and that scene was darn funny! Last year I was at a networking dinner with about ten other people, and one of the guys I had just met fancied himself as a comedian of sorts. He had several canned jokes, which, frankly, were pretty good. It reminded me of the scene from Goodfellas; he was Tommy—the guy at the center of attention who thought he was the funniest person in the group. He told a few jokes, everyone laughed, and then he told a few more. We had a good time. But one of the guests I had known for a while came up to me as we were leaving and made a comment that I'll never forget. He just said: "That guy's a goofball." It wasn't meant to be flattering. The tone of the statement was dismissive and indicated that there would be no way he'd trust the wannabe comedian with his business. I let the statement sink in and realized that, even though I thought the guy was funny and fairly professional, someone else thought all the joking around was over the top and in the end unbecoming of a professional business partner. Bottom line is that you just never know how your humor will affect someone's perception of you, so be careful. To this day, though, I wish I could remember all of the guy's jokes in case I ever become a sit-down comedian (too much pressure doing stand-up these days)!

THE ZEN OF RULE 8

There's something about laughter that makes us feel more alive. I like to live as fully as possible, and looking for humor in life and enjoying the humor of others is a blessing in my life. I was trying to think about the hardest I've ever laughed. As I thought through it, there were many times when I felt I've laughed the hardest. But one time in particular jumped out at me right away. Although there are a number of great professional comedians out there, my favorite right now (and perhaps forever) is a fellow Italian and Chicagoan: Sebastian Maniscalco. If memory serves, his father comes from the same part of Sicily as my father. When I first found out about Sebastian, I started listening to everything I could find online. I would be driving in the car by myself and start cracking up. Then one of his first Netflix specials came out, and I watched it as soon as I could. Honest to God, I had to literally stop the show near the middle just to catch my breath because I was laughing so hard! I've never had that sort of experience before. It was exhilarating. I loved it. Since then, I try to go to all of his live performances when he comes to town. The feeling we get when we laugh is memorable. Look for ways to share this sort of experience and memory with other people as often as possible in appropriate ways. Everyone is better off and more alive as a result!

KEY TAKEAWAY

When appropriate, infuse tasteful humor into a conversation to engender feelings of acceptance and happiness in the other person.

Rule 9

Identify Shared Interests to Emphasize Like-Mindedness

Your passions are a bit like your fingerprints:
Everybody has them; everybody's are different.
One's passions may just be a guidebook to one's life.

—Nick Woodman (American businessman)

DO THIS!

If you have a passion or hobby, share it with people, especially if they have never experienced it before.

WHY?

We are drawn to people who are like-minded.[1] In fact, common life points among us—shared beliefs, activities, and interests—have been shown to increase the frequency of our online social interactions, which, in turn, increases the connectedness among us as human

---

[1] Angela J. Bahns et al. "Similarity in Relationships as Niche Construction: Choice, Stability, and Influence Within Dyads in a Free Choice Environment," *Journal of Personality and Social Psychology* (2016), DOI: 10.1037/pspp0000088.

beings.[2] Shared interests of any kind (e.g., a passion for music, comedy, travel, photography, hunting, dancing, or visiting museums) can establish and enhance relationships. "Birds of a feather absolutely flock together," says relationship expert and author Ty Tashiro. "Shared interests are a strong predictor of who you're attracted to because the more you have in common with someone, the more points of attraction exist between you."[3]

Perhaps more important than the general notion that shared interests are important to relationship-building is the idea that sharing *rare* interests are even more effective in connecting people.[4] Certainly bonding over common traits is good, but doing so over unique, unusual, or otherwise uncommon ones enhances interpersonal attraction.[5] Think through the interests you have, and try to focus on those that may be more uncommon. Then welcome others into that world by offering to share those interests with them.

And as you are developing a relationship with someone, practice active listening (Rule 4) to identify interests that person has, especially those that might be more unusual or unique, and express a sincere interest in them—so long as you are truly and genuinely interested. By expressing that sort of interest, you invite the other person to welcome you into his or her special world—into that individual's passion. This brings you closer to that person and helps

---

[2] Emanuel Sanchiz, Francisco Ibarra, Svetlana Nikitina, Marcos Baez and Fabio Casati, "What Makes People Bond?: A Study on Social Interactions and Common Life Points on Facebook," 26-30. 10.1109/CTS.2016.0024.

[3] Gabrielle Gresge, "Having This in Common Can Make Your Relationship Better," https://www.brit.co/shared-interests-makes-relationships-better/.

[4] Hans Alves, "Sharing Rare Attitudes Attracts." *Personality and Social Psychology Bulletin* 44, no. 8 (2018): 1270–83.

[5] Id.

make your relationship more unique and more difficult for that person to replace. That increases and strengthens the bond between you.

A FEW TIPS ABOUT RULE 9

- The power of Rule 9 is in the degree of your passion or interest in your hobby. Think about what you really enjoy doing *more than anything else*. Whatever it is, people will be motivated and enthused by your passion and strong interest.

- Time the invitation into your passion or hobby appropriately. If you are knee-deep in a conversation about a serious topic, it might not be the best time to simply switch topics without warning and suggest you go hiking. Be patient and wait for the right opening.

- Remember that not everyone will be receptive to your personal passions or hobbies. If you're into heavy metal music, and you know the other person only listens to jazz, don't be surprised if he or she declines your offer to go to the next Metallica concert.

- If you don't have a hobby, think about what you enjoy doing and start a hobby around it. For example, if you enjoy driving, join a car club. Then invite someone to join you at club events, maybe a race around the track!

- Another way to get the maximum benefit of Rule 9 is to express a sincere interest in the other person's passions and hobbies. If he or she is into archery and you've never tried it (and would sincerely like to), then ask if you can join sometime.

TRAIN WRECK: WHEN RULE 9 DERAILS

Very early on in my career as an attorney (as the rules in this book were evolving in my mind and life), I invited a potential client out to a jazz club for dinner and drinks. My musical tastes are diverse—from classical to heavy metal—but I have a soft spot for jazz because that was the genre I played the most as a kid in school bands. My guest accepted my invitation somewhat reluctantly, making clear he was not a jazz fan. I reassured him that, if he just came along, I was confident he would enjoy it and change his perspective on the genre. Well . . . not ten minutes into the performance, I glanced over and saw he was ready to jump out of his seat. He hated it! I felt like I had forced the situation and hadn't thought through how the situation could backfire. He was nice enough and didn't make me feel bad. But I could tell he wanted to get the heck out of there. I suggested quickly that we watch a game at a nearby sports bar and grab beers instead. He was more than willing to move on. Here's the moral of the story: suggest someone share in your passions and hobbies with kid gloves. Tread carefully, listen to someone's response when you extend an invitation, and follow the cues as to whether there is real interest or not.

THE ZEN OF RULE 9

One of my deepest passions in life is music. I started playing the drums when I was five years old and also picked up the guitar in high school. Although I don't fit into my black leather stage pants from high school anymore (side note: cut up, the pants these days make great shammy towels for washing the car!), I still feel the music in my bones every day of my life. One of my favorite things to do is go see live music. I enjoy going with family, friends, clients, and even by myself if no one else can make it. Perhaps the most important show I attended was with my father shortly before he passed away. I had planned to go with a buddy of mine, but he got sick and couldn't make it. It was last minute and none of my other closer friends were available. So I asked my dad, "Hey, Dad, want to go to the Motley Crue concert with me tonight?" Without hesitation, he accepted the invitation and in no time Vince, Nikki, Mick, and Tommy were "smokin' in the boys room!" (Side note: their cover of the 1973 Brownsville Station classic song is awesome! Highly recommend it.) I remember looking over to my father and realizing how cool it was that he wanted to go with me and how much I appreciated him having mercy on my desperate soul that night. There was a connection between us that I hadn't felt before as we enjoyed the show. Think about someone you care about and go see one of your favorite artists together—just like that. Take note of the feeling you have when you share your passion for music with someone you care about. It's priceless.

KEY TAKEAWAY

Welcome people into your world by inviting them to share in your passions and hobbies, and look for opportunities to share the interests of others.

Rule 10

Harness Emotional Intelligence to Effectively Navigate Social Interactions

*Emotional intelligence . . . shapes our interactions
with others and our understanding of ourselves.
It defines how and what we learn; it allows us to set priorities;
it determines the majority of our daily actions.*

—Joshua Freedman
(Author and specialist on emotional intelligence)

DO THIS!

Arm yourself with emotional intelligence.

WHY?

Emotional intelligence—the ability to perceive, appraise, and express emotions accurately and adaptively—is intuitive to some but can be learned by anyone. A number of studies have proven the many benefits of emotional intelligence, including, perhaps most importantly, the fact that "emotional intelligence is highly associated with happiness."[1] The benefits of higher emotional intelligence are endless and may be more important than intelligence quotient (IQ) in predicting success in life. Daniel Goleman, leading authority on emotional intelligence, reports that IQ may be responsible for only about 20 percent of our success, with emotional intelligence accounting for more of our success throughout our lives.[2]

The most relevant benefit of emotional intelligence in the context of this book is an increased potential for better relationships.[3] In a 2001 study, people with higher scores for emotional intelligence were found to have higher scores for close and affectionate relationships.[4] The same study also determined that we anticipate better relationships with people whom we perceive as having emotional intelligence.[5] So by being sensitive to the concept of emotional intelligence in our conversations with people, and harnessing the strength of emotional intelligence, we both increase the likelihood of having better relationships with them and allow others to expect a better relationship with us—creating a win-win scenario for both people.

Luckily, emotional intelligence can be improved at any point in life.[6] Here are just a few ways to develop emotional intelligence.

---

[1] Reuven Bar-On, "Emotional Intelligence: An Integral Part of Positive Psychology," *South African Journal of Psychology*, 40, no. 1 (March 2010), 54–62.

[2] Daniel Goleman, *Emotional Intelligence* (New York: Bantam Books, 1995).

[3] Nicola S. Schutte, John M. Malouff, Chad Bobik, Tracie D. Coston, Cyndy Greeson, Christina Jedlicka, Emily Rhodes, and Greta Wendorf, "Emotional Intelligence and Interpersonal Relations," *Journal of Social Psychology*, 141, no. 4 (2001), pp. 523–536.

[4] Id.

[5] Id.

[6] D. Goleman Liderazgo, *El poder de la inteligencia emocional* (Barcelona, Spain: B de books, 2014).

Identify your negative emotions with the goal of trying to manage them better.[7] Assess yourself objectively and look into your actions from a bird's eye view by challenging your thoughts on a regular basis (e.g., why are you thinking about something in a particular way?).[8] Focus on the right or best way to tell others how you feel and why you feel that way.[9] Work on ways to manage and reduce stress in your life.[10] Practice empathy in every conversation by putting yourself in the other person's shoes and seeing things from that individual's perspective.[11] There are a ton of resources available online and otherwise to more formally improve your emotional intelligence, which will ultimately increase the strength of your relationships.

A FEW TIPS ABOUT RULE 10

- When you're speaking to someone, simply be more mindful of how you feel about what you're saying and better observe how the other person is reacting to you. The same is true to staying in touch with your feelings about what the other person says to you.

- If there's ever a stressful situation or potential conflict with people, never "take the bait" and react how many people react (i.e., with a purely knee-jerk emotional reaction). Take a step back before responding.

---

[7] Madhuleena Roy Chowdhury, "How To Improve Emotional Intelligence Through Training," https://positivepsychology.com/emotional-intelligence-training/.

[8] Id.

[9] Id.

[10] Id.

[11] Id.

- Remember to practice your active listening skills (Rule 4) and empathize with what the other person is saying. If you do this, you will increase your ability to measure both your emotions and the other person's, which will allow you to communicate most effectively.

- Always be positive, even in the wake of potential negativity. Take a break from a conversation, if necessary, to put things in perspective and come back to the situation refreshed and with a positive attitude.

- Use leadership skills to guide a conversation in a productive way, avoiding distractions around unnecessary disagreements (Rule 14) and strategically handling polarizing topics (Rule 15). Redirect the conversation in a way to accomplish the goals of both people.

TRAIN WRECK: WHEN RULE 10 DERAILS

"Don't stand, don't stand so, don't stand so close to me." You know that The Police song. It's common sense, right? Don't stand too close to someone. It's awkward and, frankly, suggests low emotional intelligence. Empathy for the other person is absent—no one wants their personal space invaded in a social setting. How about sitting too close to someone? I was finishing up a business lunch one day a few months ago and, before I left, noticed one of my clients sitting at a high top in the bar area. She was near the window, and there were four other high-top chairs around the table. She was with a man. And he was literally sitting elbow-to-elbow with her, in the chair next to her. The other three chairs—spread generously around the balance of the table—were empty. I wanted to say hi to my client before I left, so I went over to her table. She introduced me, and they, too, were there for a business lunch (they were not dating). The entire time I was speaking with them I was completely distracted by the distance (or lack of distance) between them. It simply didn't make sense. Too close. But why? Next time I spoke with my client I had to ask. Apparently, she had sat down first, and when he came in, he sat down where I had seen him. She didn't want to make him feel bad by asking him to move further away (good display of emotional intelligence on my client's part). To this day, I don't get it. Anyone with a semblance of emotional intelligence would have not sat so close. It demonstrated that the guy lacked a basic element of emotional intelligence, namely empathy for others. He either didn't understand how that sort of proximity would make my client feel (i.e., low emotional intelligence), or he did know (even worse). Now, every time I hear that Police song, the words are a tad different in my head: "Don't sit so, don't sit so, don't sit so close to me."

THE ZEN OF RULE 10

A number of years ago, a buddy and I had gone to a hockey game, and afterwards we decided to go to a popular club in Chicago. It was where all the cool people went, and we had never seen any cool people, so we were quite curious as to what they looked like, if they would notice us, etc. We went to this club because one of my other friends had just become a bouncer for the place and was working the door that night. The line to get in was a proverbial mile long. As we approached, I saw one of my clients in line with one of his buddies. Turns out they had been waiting for a while and the line wasn't moving. We chatted with my bouncer friend, and he offered to get my friend and me in the club without waiting. I asked if we could also get my client in with his buddy, but the place was packed and the bouncer only felt comfortable getting two more in at the time. My client said, go ahead, but I turned to my bouncer friend and told him we'd just wait. And so we waited—forever! I just couldn't leave my client and buddy standing there while we went in. It felt wrong, and I'd have been miserable all night thinking about it. Although my client said it was okay, I knew it wasn't right. I didn't want him to feel bad or left out. To this day, he and I are very close, and he continues to honor me with a lot of legal business. Some might say going in and leaving him there would not have been such a big deal. But it was to me. And I feel good about it to this day. Think ahead and put yourself in someone's shoes before acting. You won't regret it.

KEY TAKEAWAY

Practice perceiving, appraising, and expressing emotions accurately and adaptively in your interactions with others.

Rule 11

Admit Mistakes and Earn Trust and Respect

Not admitting a mistake is a bigger mistake.
—Robert Half (Entrepreneur)

DO THIS!

If you make a mistake, admit it and make it right.

WHY?

We are not infallible. We make mistakes. And when we do in a relationship, we need to be mindful of the power of admitting those mistakes. No one wants us to run for the proverbial hills when we make a mistake. They want us to own up to it and try to make things right. We earn trust and respect that way—two important elements of any strong relationship. Of course, when we admit a mistake, it's embarrassing—a seemingly negative result.

But one study found that the result is actually the opposite.[1] UC Berkeley social psychologist Robb Willer, a coauthor of the study, has

---

[1] Matthew Feinberg, Robb Willer, Dacher Keltner, "Flustered and Faithful: Embarrassment as a Signal of Prosociality," *Journal of Personality and Social Psychology*, 2011, DOI: 10.1037/a0025403.

stated that "[e]mbarrassment is one emotional signature of a person to whom you can entrust valuable resources. It's part of the social glue that fosters trust and cooperation in everyday life."[2] Matthew Feinberg, a doctoral student in psychology at UC Berkeley and lead author of the study, asserts that people want to affiliate with us more and trust us more when we admit mistakes.[3]

Whether in our personal lives or in business, we need to harness the power of embarrassment in building relationships. Being embarrassed is not the best feeling in the world, but keep in mind its benefits. Others will find you more trustworthy and have more respect for you. They will want to affiliate with you and be your friend or business partner. It conveys confidence and inner strength to people and gives them confidence in you for the long-term—a nice byproduct of a mistake you likely wish never happened, namely turning what is a negative into a positive.

A FEW TIPS ABOUT RULE 11

- Admit your mistakes right away. If the other person finds out you did something wrong and realized you had the opportunity to admit it but didn't, you'll be perceived as sneaky, disrespectful, or simply weak and less than confident.

- The vast majority of the time the damage from your mistake is not the end of the world. So do whatever you can to make it right. Righting a wrong may take your time or your money or a combination of both. It's worth it.

---

[2] Yasmin Anwar, "Easily Embarrassed? Study Finds People Will Trust You More," https://news.berkeley.edu/2011/09/28/easily-embarrassed/.
[3] Id.

- When you make a mistake, apologize with the utmost sincerity. A heartfelt apology goes a long way to repair any damage that may have been done. In many cases, an apology is all the other person wants to repair the relationship.

- If you could have avoided the mistake (which is the case most often), identify what you could have done differently to have avoided the situation to begin with. Go back and think through the steps leading up to the mistake. What could you have done differently?

- If the other person is the one who made a mistake, then accept his or her apology and move on. Remember, none of us is perfect. When you accept an apology, the other person feels better, accepted, and is willing to reward you with loyalty in return.

TRAIN WRECK: WHEN RULE 11 DERAILS

I should have called this particular section "Turbulence: When Rule 11 Flies Off the Grid." On a flight to Las Vegas recently, the flight attendant unintentionally spilled a cup of water all over the passenger in front of me. I felt bad for the woman but figured that the flight attendant would apologize. Well, she did apologize, but then added, "But it wasn't my fault." Mind you, there was no turbulence, and it was an honest mistake. If she had just said, "I'm sorry," and left it at that, I'm confident the passenger would have simply let it go. After another half-hour or so, the same flight attendant came through the aisle and collected trash from the passengers. She took a large cup that looked like it was half-filled with soda from the person across the aisle but in the row in front of us, and when she tried placing it into the plastic bag, the cup dropped on top of the woman in front of me—yes, the same woman from the first spill—and out came the rest of the soda all over that passenger! I couldn't believe that had happened to this passenger twice. Again, the flight attendant apologized, but then added, "But it's not my fault. It just fell." Needless to say, the person in front of me was less than pleased with the excuse. The flight attendant was not at all interested in trying to develop or maintain a cordial relationship with the passenger. And though it did not happen to me, I felt really bad for the passenger in front of me, and my respect for the flight attendant was essentially nonexistent based on her failure to take full responsibility for her mistakes. Icing on the cake: as we were getting ready to land, I spilled what was left of the water in my cup on my leg! And yes, I did apologize to myself—fully and unequivocally.

THE ZEN OF RULE 11

As much as I'd like to consider myself a great parent to my four kids, I am flawed. Though I try my best, I've made more than a few mistakes over the years. It's tough being a good parent, let alone a perfect one. I remember too many times when the kids were very young and it was really stressful. I don't know how my wife did it all day every day when they were that young. (Frankly, I don't know how my parents survived raising me!) Was I short with my kids sometimes? Impatient? Did I raise my voice? Shut down occasionally? Say things I probably shouldn't have said with the tone I used? Yes to all of these questions. But did I learn from each and every one of those situations? Yes. Did I change my approach over the years as I matured as a parent? Yes. Do I consider myself a better parent and man because of having made some mistakes as a parent? Most definitely. Why? Because I learned from them. See, it's okay to make mistakes sometimes. The more important thing is how we learn from them and adapt for the future. That's the true measure of a person. There's a hidden reward in a mistake. It's the revelation of our humanity—our imperfection—and the gift we give ourselves afterwards when we allow ourselves to learn from that mistake and hopefully make the world a better place. Give yourself this gift. What I do not regret as I made those mistakes with the kids is telling them I loved them every chance I got—and I love still being able to do so!

KEY TAKEAWAY

We all make mistakes; admit them.

Rule 12

Be Confident, Be Compelling

Confidence is the most beautiful thing you can possess.
—Sabrina Carpenter (American singer)

DO THIS!

Convey your confidence to people and they will be more confident in the relationship.

WHY?

While it would seem to make sense that confidence would be a very attractive trait to others, the research proves it.[1] One reason why confidence is so attractive is that it quickly and efficiently conveys a perception of our value to others.[2] A confident person is perceived as competent, driven, and kind—qualities we want in a partner, whether in our personal lives or in business. In fact, being slightly

---

[1] B. P. Buunk, P. Dijkstra, D. Fetchenhauer and D. T. Kenrick, "Age and Gender Differences in Mate Selection Criteria for Various Involvement Levels," *Personal Relationship* 9 (2002): 271-278, http://dx.doi.org/10.1111/1475-6811.00018.

[2] Sean Murphy, "The Attractiveness of Confidence," https://www.spsp.org/news-center/blog/romanticconfidence.

overconfident (if we can avoid coming across as arrogant) can even give us an edge in fostering a positive perception of ourselves by others.[3]

Especially with first impressions, which have been known to last for months,[4] it is important to convey traits such as competence, personal drive, and kindness as efficiently as possible. Being confident in yourself during a first encounter can immediately help convey those desired traits to the other person in a lasting way. Remember the underlying goal of relationship development—connecting in a meaningful way with another person. If someone judges you as solid, competent, and capable, that individual is more likely to consider you a value-add to his or her life or business. Consider the opposite: if you convey low self-esteem and lack of trust in your own abilities, then why should anyone else have confidence in you? Such a negative perception will naturally result in the other person's having less confidence in you and in your potential relationship.

Even if you do not fancy yourself as the most confident person in the world, the good news is that confidence can be improved—you can learn to manage it better and make it more resilient.[5] Use these simple tricks to enhance your confidence: practice maintaining a confident posture for short periods of time (i.e., two minutes);

---

[3] Sean Murphy et al. "The Role of Overconfidence in Romantic Desirability and Competition." *Personality & social psychology bulletin* 41, no. 8 (2015): 1036-52, doi:10.1177/0146167215588754.

[4] G. Gunaydin, E. Selcuk and V. Zayas, "Impressions Based on a Portrait Predict, 1-month Later, Impressions Following a Live Interaction," *Social Psychological and Personality Science* 8 (2017): 36–44.

[5] Alyssa Dver, "Inspiring Confidence in Yourself and Others," (2015), 10.13140 /RG.2.1.4388.6567.

remember a success you had before facing a challenge; try reframing your anxiety as enthusiasm; acknowledge your emotions out loud (i.e., telling someone you're nervous about something before doing it); and use words of support for yourself like you'd articulate them to a friend.[6]

A FEW TIPS ABOUT RULE 12

- Make a list of your past successes that somehow relate to the type of relationship you're developing. In the romantic context, if you've had healthy and enjoyable relationships in the past, consider what made them successful.

- Tell someone a story about a past success that will give that person comfort that he or she can have that type of relationship with you as well. If you were part of a business deal where you and your partner made lots of money, share that information.

- Be careful not to be too overconfident. Slightly overconfident can be very helpful in conveying your confidence to others, but never come off as arrogant. Arrogance is a turn-off and will cause others to push back.

- Remember that for many people confidence is not very natural. It is learned, practiced, and developed over time with more and more successes. Success breeds more confidence in our abilities. Step up to the plate as much as possible, and give yourself the opportunity to succeed.

---

[6] Pau Navarro, "5 Ways to Feel More Confident, According to Science," https://www.entrepreneur.com/article/366229.

- Create a mantra you can say to yourself in any situation where you need to be as confident as possible. Perhaps something like, "I've done this a million times; now one more." Or simply, "I can do this." Command yourself to confidence.

TRAIN WRECK: WHEN RULE 12 DERAILS

In my varied business dealings over the years, I have met some of the smartest, most admirable, and professional people in my life. I am pleased to witness people who have the utmost level of talent carry themselves with grace and modesty. Unfortunately, there have been a few exceptions to my overall positive experiences. Several years ago, I was involved in interviewing a service provider for a client in connection with an incredibly difficult substantive issue. I hadn't known the person prior to the initial call; he was referred to us by a newer business contact of a friend of mine. As soon as the guy started talking, I was thinking words like "pompous," "egotistical," and "cocky." As he spoke with deep knowledge of his profession, his tone was disrespectful and demeaning. He was confident alright, but *way* overconfident. His confidence morphed quite instantly into leaving a sour taste in my mouth. Not only did he think he was the smartest person in the room, but the smartest person who ever lived. Frankly, I was embarrassed for him—not a great start to a potential relationship. It was as if he didn't realize we had other choices for the assignment. Needless to say, he didn't get the gig. As it turned out, we picked another equally, if not more qualified, professional who has been rewarded with years of loyalty from my client and me.

THE ZEN OF RULE 12

Confidence is tied to experience. After decades in business, I feel that I've reached a point in my career where I'm very confident in developing new client relationships. It wasn't always that way. When I first started out in the legal profession, I was blessed with an early and, frankly, surprising success. One of my college professors, who had become a friend, called me literally the first week after I had passed the bar exam. He had a small business and needed a modest contract drafted. Although I did the job, my handling of the representation was less than elegant. I had never dealt with one of my own clients before. I struggled with what to say, how to say it, and how to manage the relationship. As I started to go out to develop new business from other potential clients, I was nervous, anxious, and far from confident. On the one hand, it felt unnatural, but on the other hand, there was something inside me that felt good about it. I knew that if I kept getting experience with new clients, I'd feel more confident about things. And that's exactly what happened. It would have been easy to jump ship and give up the pursuit of my own book of business and the rewards that come with it. But I stayed the course in light of my lack of confidence and, over time, things improved. Stay with something and pat yourself on the back during the tough times as you're getting experience with it. Things will get better and easier, and you'll come out the other side more confident and much happier as a result.

KEY TAKEAWAY

Confidence is key to success in getting others to be confident about your relationship with them.

Rule 13

Care Through Your Actions

The simple act of caring is heroic.
—Edward Albert (American actor)

DO THIS!

Sincerely care about people and take action to let them know it.

WHY?

We might often consider our empathy for people as a form of caring about them. "Feeling someone's pain" is most certainly important in relationship development, as it allows us to put ourselves in someone else's shoes, giving us a better understanding of that person. But that feeling we have is internal to us. It doesn't necessarily mean we feel motivated to do something about it—to act. Taking actions is critical to the concept of caring, the essence of Rule 13. When you care about someone, you have an emotional investment in that person's well-being, and that investment is characterized by a strong motivation to take some sort of action that will benefit that person.[1]

---

[1] Saul J. Weiner and Simon Auster. "From Empathy to Caring: Defining the Ideal Approach to a Healing Relationship." *The Yale Journal of Biology and Medicine* 80, no. 3 (2007): 123-30.

When we care for someone, we practice active listening (Rule 4) during our conversations with that person, ask pointed questions to give us creative ways to help him or her, and then we take actions directly addressing that individual's issues, needs, or problems.[2] During this process, people are left with a perception that we are there for them (which we are) and that we will take concrete actions (hopefully, creating solutions) to help them overcome whatever roadblocks are in front of them. As a result, they will be very appreciative, and the bond of the relationship gets stronger.

The perception of caring—or perception of social support (PSS)—is compelling to people and is a relationship enhancer because it serves as a protector and a buffer to stress.[3] It allows people to deal better with their anxiety, fears, and sadness.[4] This is equally applicable in a business and non-business setting. If you are in a romantic relationship and your partner is dealing with a stressful situation, listen, ask questions about the situation, and take some concrete action to help your partner. Your actions make it easier for your partner to cope with the stress and, in turn, they bring that person closer to you. The same concept can be applied in a business setting when you take actions to help resolve a business problem, satisfy business needs, or accomplish a business goal. Those actions help protect your business partner and the trust and confidence in the relationship is naturally enhanced.

---

[2] Id.

[3] Oh et al., "The Effect of Perceived Social Support on Chemotherapy-related Symptoms in Patients with Breast Cancer: A Prospective Observational Study." *Journal of Psychosomatic Research*, 130 (March 2020), doi:10.1016/j.psychores .2019.109911.

[4] Id.

A FEW TIPS ABOUT RULE 13

- Make sure people know you're there for them. Actually say it: "I'm here for you—however I can help." Then listen to them, ask questions about the situation, and formulate actions you can take to help them.

- It's certainly fine to identify with the other person's problems, but don't let that feeling distract you from coming up with strategic ways you can help that individual. Getting too emotional can paralyze your objectivity if you aren't careful.

- Caring involves a continuing emotional investment in someone's well-being. It's not a one-and-done concept. It applies over time during the relationship. Think of ways to continually show you care.

- Utilize your value network (Rule 7) to take actions to show you care. It's helpful to ask for favors of friends to help others. Having a solid value network allows you to take action to help others confidently (Rule 12) and promptly when it matters most.

- You don't want to be perceived as overbearing or inattentive to the needs of people. Balance your actions in helping someone given the stage of the relationship. Doing too much too soon or not enough (when you should do more) to help someone can be damaging to the relationship.

TRAIN WRECK: WHEN RULE 13 DERAILS

Several years ago, one of my clients introduced me to a friend of his who was in career transition. I met his friend with the purpose of brainstorming people I knew who might be able provide suitable employment for her. Over the next several weeks, I introduced her to a few key contacts of mine who were perfect for her situation. Simultaneously, she had been talking to a few other people to get leads for a new job. It's always good to cast a wide net when seeking a new position, especially at high levels. Fast forward: a year later, the person landed in a great position, though not as a result of any of my introductions. She called me to let me know she had landed and expressed how much she appreciated my proactive efforts to help her find a new gig. She had found the position through a relative of hers and mentioned to me that I was one of only two people who actually tried to help her in a meaningful way. She was rueful about how a number of the others she had asked for help literally didn't lift a finger to assist her in her search. Today, I am honored to receive a great amount of work from this person—as a reward for the goodwill I had earned with my actions of caring about her situation? Perhaps, and for that I am grateful. But I didn't help her to get something back. I would have helped her no matter what. The others who didn't even try to help her are much less fortunate. They may have wanted to help, but they didn't act, and they aren't doing business with this individual now. They had the opportunity to help but chose not to, for whatever reason, or they were simply lazy. To have the chance to build sincere goodwill with someone and then to fail to act does indeed have its consequences.

THE ZEN OF RULE 13

Some of the most generous people I have ever met have been staff and volunteers for charitable organizations. There are so many people in need in this world. No matter the cause (helping people with physical health issues or mental illnesses, those in poverty, etc.), the organizations that exist to help people in need are commendable beyond description. I am humbled by the staff members of these charities who dedicate their careers to a cause or those board members who spend a ton of their precious time helping people who benefit from the charity. Serving any charitable cause in any capacity is one of the best examples of taking concrete actions to help others. Though I do not consider myself an expert in the universe, I do believe in karma. Helping others in any capacity is good for the soul and enriches us personally as a byproduct. When we help people we know personally, the feeling certainly hits home. But consider dedicating more of your time to helping people you don't know, whether through service on a charitable board or other type of volunteer work. What if *we* needed the help? What if we don't need it now, but do someday?

KEY TAKEAWAY

Care for people by taking concrete actions that help them.

Rule 14

If You Disagree,
Search for Common Ground

Harmony makes small things grow;
lack of it makes great things decay.

—Sallust (Roman historian)

DO THIS!

Work hard to maintain harmony in your communications with people.

WHY?

Instead of disagreeing, be strategic in how to handle tough topics where you and your conversation partner may have a difference of opinion. Disagreement can easily evolve into an argument, and that sort of disharmony is a great way to sour an otherwise mutually beneficial relationship. Understanding "the illusion of explanatory depth" is critical to strategically navigating areas of potential disagreement. The illusion of explanatory depth means that we confuse a shallow familiarity with general concepts for real, in-depth knowledge.[1] Although we do not have deep knowledge of the details of the topic, we oftentimes believe we can explain the topic adequately, but when pressed for an explanation about our position on the topic, our explanations are often vague and incoherent.[2]

Why is understanding the illusion of explanatory depth important for relationship building? It's important because, instead of "taking the bait," we have the wisdom to take a step back and remember that unless the person is an expert on a topic, that person's knowledge about that topic likely lacks expert depth *as yours likely does* (assuming you are not an expert). If you allow the conversation to continue in an energized way around opinions that lack depth, there will never be resolution. People tend to dig in and try to avoid embarrassment by being proven wrong.

The alternative to participating in a discussion where each party is simply defending his or her position is to use a few simple tricks to recharacterize the entire conversation. For example, try to ask the other person to explain how his or her position would practicably play out in real life, using real examples.[3] If you get the sense that the stated position would fail if such a practical explanation is provided, the other person might just become more moderate in his or her opinion, having realized that the position they took is either unrealistic or unexplainable with real life examples. If you are trying to cast

[1] Philip M. Fernbach, et al., "Political Extremism Is Supported by an Illusion of Understanding." *Psychological Science* 24, no. 6 (2013): 939-46, doi:10.1177/0956797612464058.

[2] Id.

[3] David Robson, "The Science of Influencing People: Six Ways to Win an Argument," https://www.theguardian.com/science/2019/jun/30/the-science-of-influencing-people-six-ways-to-win-an-argument.

doubt on what you believe is false, try filling the gaps in the other person's understanding with a convincing, coherent story—one filled with undeniable facts.[4] Maybe reframe the entire discussion by finding something on which you both can agree and focusing on that during your conversation. Appealing to the broader values of a person, as opposed to the specific issue around which there is potential disagreement, diffuses the situation and gets both people focused on areas of agreement.[5] If you go down a rabbit hole of disagreement, your relationship is at serious risk of damage, perhaps forever.

A FEW TIPS ABOUT RULE 14

- Avoid the temptation to prove yourself right all the time. Pride can get in the way of relationships. While it might feel good if you argue and prove to the other person that he or she is wrong, no one wants to walk away from the situation feeling foolish.

- We're all victim to the illusion of explanatory depth and could very well be relying on a weak position on a topic. This will only motivate the other person to dig in and commit to fighting. If you're wrong or your position is flimsy, avoid an unnecessary disagreement.

- It's perfectly fine to agree to disagree. No two people are ever going to agree on everything. Agreeing all the time on everything would be terribly boring for most of us. We all have different lenses through which we view the world and form

---

[4] Id.
[5] Id.

opinions. We should appreciate and respect the differences between us.

- Look for areas of agreement. Agree when you can. Avoid saying things like, "No, I don't think so," or "I think you're wrong." Someone can interpret those statements as unwelcome challenges to his or her intelligence or values.

- Approach a topic of potential disagreement with a sense of calm, empathy, and respect for the other person. Feel free to state your opinion, but avoid unnecessary negativity by using the strategies noted in this Rule 14.

TRAIN WRECK: WHEN RULE 14 DERAILS

I have always enjoyed negotiating deals and advocating on behalf of my clients. Representing great clients (most of which have become my personal friends) is a true honor, and their interests are paramount. During a negotiation, I work hard to protect my client and, provided the terms of the deal are acceptable, to get the deal done. Over the years, I have encountered a handful of other attorneys who love to disagree on just about everything. Those are the deals that either die or become so difficult to complete that it becomes a terribly inefficient process for both clients. My approach is to advocate and, if there is an honest difference of perspective in light of the parties' respective interests, find a way to compromise, if possible. If the other attorney is simply disagreeing with everything without even attempting to compromise on tough issues, then no matter how hard I try to be reasonable and find a middle ground, the deal is at risk. The best way to handle honest disagreements is to redirect the conversation to shared interests and common ground, which almost always exists. Except in rare situations, that approach is a pathway to compromise and a deal. Stubbornness (in some cases to avoid being considered "wrong") can rip a deal—a relationship—right off the tracks.

THE ZEN OF RULE 14

In law school, one of my favorite courses was alternative dispute resolution (ADR). ADR is an attempt to avoid litigation, which can be costly, time-consuming, and painful in many other ways. One form of ADR is mediation. Mediation is a process where a third party—a "mediator"—attempts to get both sides to find common ground and settle a dispute. A typical mediation might involve the mediator meeting with each side separately and hearing them out. The mediator would then shuffle between the sides and attempt to bring back information that is intended and presented in a way to encourage compromise. The process of getting to yes (the title of a great book about negotiation by the way[6]) is focused on getting to the real interests of the parties—what they care about most. In the great majority of cases, a talented mediator can get the parties to compromise and get to a yes on a settlement. Like most settlements, neither side gets everything it wants, but each usually gets what it really needs. Next time you're in a potential disagreement with someone, be your own mediator. Try to identify what the other person really cares about and be honest with what you really care about. Find ways to compromise and get to a peaceful resolution. Mediate your way to yes!

---

[6] Roger Fisher, William Ury and Bruce Patton, *Getting to Yes: Negotiating Agreement Without Giving In*, 3rd ed., rev. ed. (New York: Penguin, 2011).

KEY TAKEAWAY

Creatively put a positive spin on areas of potential disagreement, and try to avoid any disagreement altogether.

Rule 15

Be Strategic About Polarizing Topics

The emotional brain responds to an event more quickly than the thinking brain.

—Daniel Goleman (Author and science journalist)

DO THIS!

Avoid topics that tend to charge someone's emotions, especially a person you've just met.

WHY?

When you first meet someone, there is typically a fair amount of small talk where each person is feeling out the other and getting a sense as to whether they like the other individual. During this important time in the relationship, avoid sensitive topics that might be emotional triggers for people. We all have different sensitivities to various topics, and when you first meet someone, you really don't know that person's unique variety of sensitivities. So stick to topics that are universally accepted as nonconfrontational; otherwise, the other person is at risk of getting emotionally off-kilter for no good reason.

Some of the topics to avoid include politics, religion, sex, finances, death, appearance, personal gossip, offensive jokes, health, narrow topics around which most people might not be well-versed, and past relationships.[1] People tend to have strong views about some of these topics, or they might give rise to bad memories or feelings, or otherwise they might make people uncomfortable. Instead, stick to topics such as arts and entertainment, weather, sports, family, food, work, celebrity gossip, travel, hobbies, and hometowns.[2]

After you get to know someone, it is more appropriate to tackle more difficult topics because there is an underlying level of built-up respect in the relationship. It is almost inevitable to avoid all tough topics, and it may not be healthy to do so. In many cases, when people *are* able to manage discussions over difficult topics, the relationship is strengthened. If dealing with a polarizing topic, make an effort to honestly communicate when you disagree, use a positive style of talking about tough topics, and view yourself as a team when working through discussions around otherwise difficult topics.[3]

A FEW TIPS ABOUT RULE 15

- Remember that some people like to bring up polarizing topics during small talk. They might be looking to see how you react,

---

[1] Arlin Cuncic, "10 Best and Worst Small Talk Topics," https://www.verywellmind.com/small-talk-topics-3024421.

[2] Id.

[3] P. Gray and D. F. Bjorklund, *Psychology*, 8th ed., (Worth Publishers, 2018): 485.

or they may simply like talking about those topics. Look for ways to redirect the conversation in a respectful way.

- If your gut tells you that engaging in a conversation around a potentially polarizing topic would be harmless, then by all means have that discussion. The idea behind Rule 15 is to avoid the possibility of unnecessary friction.

- If a tough topic is raised by the other person that is an emotional trigger for you, then take a deep breath and don't respond right away. Use your emotional intelligence (Rule 9). Give yourself a chance to think about a dignified response that can redirect the conversation.

- It's perfectly okay to let someone know that you feel uncomfortable talking about a topic. There's no requirement that you sit through a conversation about a loaded topic if you don't want to. But let the other person know that in a respectful way (Rule 17).

- As you get to know someone more, you'll inevitably talk about all sorts of topics, including difficult ones. Always address the other person with respect (Rule 17) and empathy. Work together to maintain good rapport (Rule 20).

TRAIN WRECK: WHEN RULE 15 DERAILS

Reasonable people will have different opinions about a host of political issues. It is one thing to passionately advocate for an issue, but it's quite another thing to burn a personal bridge over it. It has become quite common (unfortunately) to hear about friends or family members who end their relationships over politics. Over dinner with one of my friends and several newer acquaintances, I literally witnessed the end of a friendship before it even started—over politics. Although the two people involved had just met, they seemed to get along the entire dinner. I envisioned their becoming good friends. But the political environment had gotten both people so energized over their respective positions that they escalated the conversation into a shouting match. After a while, one of them got up and left the restaurant. Everyone else at the table that night (including me) felt like crawling into a hole because we were so uncomfortable. Though it has been more than four years since their argument, they have yet to speak again—over one heated political discussion. I would guess that you know one or more people who have suffered in their relationships over political disagreements with others. And you may have met someone for the first time who jumps into politics out of the gate, asking you who you voted for or what you think about a very controversial political issue. Not only are those questions uncomfortable for most people, they're, frankly, inappropriate when first meeting someone. Once you get to know someone, then it's okay to venture deeper into political waters, but only with the utmost respect for someone's viewpoint. And if you must engage in political conversations in a restaurant, do yourself and everyone else a favor: wait until after dessert.

THE ZEN OF RULE 15

Even in light of the emotionally charged political environment we might find ourselves in every so often, I am confident that people can have calm and intelligent discussions about tough political issues. My confidence stems in large part from conversations I used to have with one of my very best lifetime friends. We met in law school at lunch during our first year. How we started chatting is a story for another day. (If we ever meet, ask me to tell you the story—it's quite humorous). When our conversations turned to politics, we realized we were on the exact opposite sides of the political spectrum. But we also soon realized that we really enjoyed our conversations. He would calmly and articulately state his position, and then I would do the same. We'd go back and forth sometimes for hours, trying to convince the other he was wrong. The more we discussed politics, the more each of us gained respect for the other. We didn't fight or try to make the other person feel foolish. We didn't ignore the reasonableness of the other person's logic even if our guts told us we were still right. As a result, we each learned a lot. Our political beliefs have evolved over time, with each of us being much less stubborn in our views (actually not stubborn at all; we're just still convinced we're each right!). I often think back to those days and wish people today could feel the blessing of having great, eye-opening discussions about very important political topics like I had with my old friend. Let's all do each other a favor: when we talk politics, let's show the utmost respect for others and try to understand where they're coming from. There's plenty of room for compromise and peace.

KEY TAKEAWAY

Stick to easy topics when first meeting people.

Rule 16

Remember the 50/50 Listen/Speak Dynamic in Conversations

You aren't learning anything when you're talking.
—Lyndon B. Johnson (36th U.S. President)

DO THIS!

Speak 50% of the time; let the other person speak 50% of the time.

WHY?

We all have an impulse to survive and flourish, and by talking about ourselves, we help satisfy that impulse.[1] We tend to spend 60% of our conversations talking about ourselves, 80% when chatting on social media.[2] Why? Because it simply feels good.[3] The problem

---

[1] Lydia Dishman, "The Science Of Why We Talk Too Much (And How To Shut Up)," https://www.fastcompany.com/3047285/the-science-of-why-we-talk-too-much-and-how-to-shut-up.

[2] Adrian F. Ward, "The Neuroscience of Everybody's Favorite Topic, Why do people spend so much time talking about themselves?" https://www.scientificamerican.com/article/the-neuroscience-of-everybody-favorite-topic-themselves/.

[3] Diana Tamir and Jason Mitchell, "Disclosing Information about the Self Is Intrinsically Rewarding," Proceedings of the National Academy of Sciences of the United States of America 109 (2012): 8038-43, 10.1073/pnas.1202129109.

is that when we are developing relationships with others, we need to learn about them, and the main way we learn is by listening. We can't learn if we're talking too much.

Another big problem with talking too much during a conversation is that people tune out and your message gets lost. The harsh reality is that human beings have dwindling attention spans, which have been measured between as many as 59 seconds, to as few as eight seconds.[4] The idea is for someone to get to know us as much as we get to know that individual (Rule 4), but if someone tunes out, the accurate reception of our self-disclosure is at risk.

Strive for about a 50/50 split during a conversation—you speak 50% of the time and the other person speaks 50% of the time. That means you need to be quiet half the time—something we may not be used to doing instinctually. "Silence is a greatly underestimated source of power. In silence, we can hear not only what is being said, but also what is not being said. In silence, it can be easier to reach the truth."[5] Let the other person talk at least half of the time. Actually, it's perfectly okay to let other people dominate the conversation, whether talking about themselves or anything else. By allowing people to satisfy the impulse noted above about why people talk a lot (i.e., the impulse to survive and flourish), they will be appreciative that you accommodated that impulse. And always remember what Dale Carnegie, author of *How to Win Friends and Influence People*, said: "Talk to someone about themselves and they'll listen for hours."

---

[4] Lydia Dishman, "The Science Of Why We Talk Too Much (And How To Shut Up)," https://www.fastcompany.com/3047285/the-science-of-why-we-talk-too-much-and-how-to-shut-up.

[5] Peter Bregman, "If You Want People to Listen, Stop Talking," https://hbr.org/2015/05/if-you-want-people-to-listen-stop-talking.

We all enjoy talking about ourselves. If people you are with want to talk about themselves, then by all means let them.

A FEW TIPS ABOUT RULE 16

- Most people will consider you self-centered or narcissistic if you talk too much. If someone thinks the relationship is going to be all about you, then there's no purpose in pursuing it. Avoid creating this perception.

- Listening to someone drone on and on is just boring. Think about the last time you were with someone who just kept talking. How did you feel? Others will feel the same way if you talk too much.

- Not letting the other person have equal time may cause resentment. No one wants to be disrespected (Rule 17), and if you don't respect someone enough to give that person at least 50% talking time, then you run the risk of alienating him or her for no good reason.

- Get a feel for someone's style as soon as possible. Not everyone is an extrovert, and he or she might desire that you lead, or even dominate, the conversation. But make sure to be respectful (Rule 17), and give the other person as much of an opportunity to speak as possible.

- If asked a question, maintain a 50/50 split talking by asking the same question back. For example, if someone asks about your kids, then ask the other person the same question and allow him or her to speak uninterrupted for at least the same amount of time.

TRAIN WRECK: WHEN RULE 16 DERAILS

Sometimes in life it's time to move on. One of my casual acquaintances for quite some time had become so narcissistic that I simply had had enough. Early on in the relationship, I saw signs of narcissism but due to our potential business relationship, I chose to let it go. Over the years, his self-absorption had gotten so bad that we couldn't get together without his dominating the conversation with—wait for it—yup, himself! About a year ago, we got together for dinner, and it started: chapter and verse about his recent vacation, his job, his wife, his kids, his recent investments, his last business trip and an upcoming one, his car, his dinner the night before, his this and his that and everything in between, wall-to-wall, side-to-side! Every time I tried to get a word in, he gave my words short shrift with a nod of his head and then started back into his self-serving commentary. I felt as if I could have walked away and he would not have even cared—now *that* would have done some serious damage to my self-esteem! After a while, I found myself not even listening to him. As he spoke, I made a mental note: don't rush back. Although I actually do really like the guy, self-absorption to such an extent during a conversation is simply not fun for me. It was time to move on from that relationship, and I have. The best thing about that day was going home and telling my dog, Prince, everything I had wanted to say at that dinner. Guess what? Not a single interruption, although I think I blatantly violated the 50/50 talking rule! Sorry, Prince.

THE ZEN OF RULE 16

As much as Rule 16 is important in developing a unique relationship with someone, there are times when I find that someone is so darn interesting that I find myself getting closer to that person the more he or she speaks. Through my network, I met a guy a number of years ago who has an incredibly interesting background. My guess is that he's at least 25 years older than me. Very well educated, world-traveled, highly intelligent, and overall one of the most interesting people I've ever met. I remember one time we were in a lounge with some other people and he started to speak. And he kept talking and talking. At first I was put off by the man, concluding that he was self-absorbed, with little regard for the thoughts of others. But as he continued, I realized I didn't want him to stop. I figured out that he was far from narcissistic. He wanted to teach us (the younger guys) about life and only wanted the best for us. I considered myself lucky to be there to listen to his wisdom and infinite knowledge. Of course, he let others speak a little, but took the opportunity to control the conversation, and we were all more than willing to let him do it. So sometimes blatant violations of the 50/50 dynamic can actually work out well. But if you are the one speaking 95% of the time, please be sure you really are as interesting as you might think you are. Personally, I could never pull that off.

KEY TAKEAWAY

Pay attention to how much you're talking during a conversation, and talk just enough given the circumstances.

Rule 17

Give Respect to Get Respect

We should all consider each other as human beings,
and we should respect each other.

—Malala Yousafzai (Pakistani activist for female education)

DO THIS!

Always treat people with respect.

WHY?

Respect—"a feeling or understanding that someone or something is important, serious, etc., and should be treated in an appropriate way"[1]—is essential to healthy relationships. Everyone wants to be respected. Actually, respect is more important to people than how much money they have.[2] A high level of respect for someone can create a strong connection, and lack of respect can kill a relationship.

---

[1] https://www.merriam-webster.com/dictionary/respect.

[2] Cameron Anderson, et al. "The local-ladder effect: social status and subjective well-being." *Psychological Science* 23, no. 7 (2012): 764-71, doi:10.1177/09567976 11434537.

When you show respect for people, you're acknowledging their value as human beings and honoring them—whether you agree with them or not. You're letting people know you care about them and aren't trying to change them.[3] And if you want others to respect you, you must show them respect.

Respect—and lack of respect—can be revealed in many ways. One simple way to think about showing maximum respect for people and avoiding being disrespectful is to follow the Golden Rule: treat others the way you want to be treated.[4] If you follow this principle, then you will always think before you speak when faced with a judgment about someone's thoughts or actions. You will not criticize someone for his or her values, religious beliefs, political views, cultural norms, and a host of other things that could eat away at respect between people if not treated properly.

A FEW TIPS ABOUT RULE 17

- You need to respect yourself. Treat yourself well and others will see that. They will acknowledge that you're the type of person that is deserving of respect. If you don't respect yourself, then why should anyone else respect you?

- If you allow people to disrespect you, then they'll likely continue to do so. You don't want to be associated with anyone who doesn't respect you. Respect is a fundamental human right, and never give up that right.

- Always think about how your words and actions will affect others. Think about how you would feel if the roles were

---

[3] https://blog.cognifit.com/respect/.
[4] https://en.wikipedia.org/wiki/Golden_Rule.

reversed. If you make someone feel unimportant or less than a serious person, the damage is done.

- Unless necessary (and usually it's not), just let comments go to the wayside instead of saying something that might be considered disrespectful by the other person. Why run the risk of insulting someone by your reaction to their heartfelt thoughts on a topic? No one wants to feel like his or her opinion is insignificant.

- Regular use of the other rules in this book is a show of respect to everyone you meet. Practice the rules while building relationships, and always remember the Golden Rule.

TRAIN WRECK: WHEN RULE 17 DERAILS

Several years ago, on our way to a college tour in Iowa, my family and I witnessed one of the most vile examples of disrespect I can remember. We had stopped at a gas station to fill up and buy some water. One of my sons asked, "Why would someone do that?" I said, "Do what?" as I looked toward where he was looking. I couldn't believe what I saw. There was a mini van parked near the edge of the gas station property by a grassy area that was atop a hill. A family of four—the parents and two small kids—were "cleaning" out their car by throwing their debris over the hill. We saw fast food bags, soda cups, dirty napkins, empty water bottles, among other things, being whipped onto the grass—in plain sight with a trash container just steps away from them! My family and I were speechless. I couldn't answer my son's question. I was literally frozen in shock. Their actions were disrespectful in so many ways. Littering is always disrespectful. And in this situation, they placed no value on the property of the gas station owner. They didn't care about other patrons of the gas station having to look at their mess. And they were essentially saying they couldn't care less about the earth. Stupidity is troubling itself, but the fact that the parents were teaching their young children to do something so disrespectful just makes me sad to this day. Disrespect can have many faces, and its effects can be long-lasting. As we pulled away, I simply answered by son's question by saying, "They don't have any respect—for themselves. We should say a prayer for them."

THE ZEN OF RULE 17

Sunday dinners at my maternal grandmother's house were part of our weekly routine. She would get up early on Sunday mornings with one goal in mind: start the gravy (yeah, we called it gravy back then—and I still do!). The gravy, meatballs, sausage, and dessert—all homemade. She bought the bread from the best baker in town. My job was to taste the pasta before she took it out of the giant pot to make sure it was cooked enough but not too much. While I waited until the pasta was done, I would "foon" (in my Italian family, that's how we referred to dipping) the bread in the gravy while it was still in the pot to make sure the gravy was ready, too. We didn't have a large immediate family. Sunday dinners usually involved six people, but she cooked for a small army! There was SO MUCH FOOD. When we all sat down to eat, we knew we'd be at the table for at least a couple hours. After the first helping, we would all be stuffed. But my grandmother would offer a second helping—of everything. No one wanted to make her feel bad by not having more. After all, she had been cooking all day. I always took a second helping. Then she started to push the third helping. By this time, I was ready for a nap. But then she'd look at me as if I had told her the food was terrible. She (like most Italian people I grew up with) identified food with love. Bottom line: there was no way I was going to refuse the third helping. (In my own defense, rarely did I eat much of it—but there was no way I was going to tell my grandmother no.) It was about respect. Respect for the fact that she spent all day cooking. Respect for the fact that she showed her love for us (in part) by feeding us. Respect for her position in the family. To this day, I think about how important respect is and how much it means to people. Treat everyone with respect, and let's change the world together. I also often think about how much I miss my grandmother—and her cooking!

KEY TAKEAWAY

Show others the respect you would like from them.

Rule 18

Say Thanks and Foster Gratitude

Take time to be kind and to say "Thank you."
—Zig Ziglar (American author)

DO THIS!

Be appreciative of people and say thank you.

WHY?

Saying thank you to someone is easy. Do it often. If someone does something nice for you, say thank you. If you receive a compliment, say thank you. Doing this strengthens relationships.[1] Gratitude makes the other person feel closer to us and more committed to the relationship.[2] Being sensitive to thanking people can really increase the level of satisfaction in a relationship.[3]

---

[1] Jess Alberts and Angela Trethewey, "Love, Honor, and Thank," https://greatergood.berkeley.edu/article/item/love_honor_thank/.

[2] N. M. Lambert, et. al. "Benefits of Expressing Gratitude: Expressing Gratitude to a Partner Changes One's View of the Relationship" *Psychological Science* 21, no. 4 (April 2010): 574-580.

[3] Sara B. Algoe, Shelly L. Gable, Natalya C. Maisel, "It's the little things: Everyday gratitude as a booster shot for romantic relationships," (Published Online May 21, 2010), https://onlinelibrary.wiley.com/doi/abs/10.1111/j.1475-6811.2010.01273.x.

When someone feels appreciated, he or she is more likely to want to show you kindness and return the favor.[4] Be mindful of when you should be thanking other people. If you ask someone to do something for you, offer up an immediate and sincere thanks. If someone you employ does a good job on a project, thank that person right away while your sentiment is fresh and timely.

Consider the power of thanking people when they least expect it. An immediate thank you is certainly important to the growth of a relationship. But thanking someone when they are not expecting it can have an even greater effect on that person. For example, if someone is a great client, send a handwritten note out of the blue, especially if you haven't talked to that person in a while, and thank your client for his or her trust in you and the business. The same can be said for non-business friends. Saying how much you are thankful for your relationship with someone in a note is a great relationship-builder. Handwritten notes of appreciation are powerful ways to demonstrate your gratitude.[5]

A FEW TIPS ABOUT RULE 18

- Think about how you feel when someone does *not* thank you for something. You never want someone to ever feel that way. People will always remember if you don't say thanks for a kind gesture.

- Thanking people with words is great, but consider other ways you can communicate your gratitude for people, such

[4] Cindy McGovern, "Why Saying 'Thank You' Matters," http://www.crownconnect.com/why-saying-thank-you-matters/.

[5] Amit Kumar and Nicholas Epley. "Undervaluing Gratitude: Expressers Misunderstand the Consequences of Showing Appreciation." *Psychological Science* (First published online: June 27, 2018), DOI: 10.1177/0956797618772506.

as buying them a gift card, taking them to dinner or to a game or concert, sending them a book, or contributing to a charity they care about.

- When you thank someone, look them in the eye (Rule 1) and smile (Rule 3). Be direct and sincere. When you connect with someone through the eyes with a smile, you will touch their emotional side and the gratitude will be more meaningful.

- Use other phrases in addition to a direct "Thank you," such as: "I won't forget this," "Truly appreciated," "I wasn't expecting that," "That is very kind of you," "That's really meaningful to me," "How can I return the favor?" "I owe you big time."

- When someone thanks *you*, acknowledge the other person's gratitude with sincerity. A simple "You're welcome" is fine. But think about how you can add some additional heartfelt gratitude of your own in response.

TRAIN WRECK: WHEN RULE 18 DERAILS

One of my most favorite things to do is help my friends build their businesses or otherwise help enrich their lives. With my worldwide network of contacts and relationships, it is rare that I cannot help people with something, whether it be making a strategic introduction to someone who can help their business or career generally, providing access to information they need, hooking them up with great concert or sporting event tickets, and so on. Recently, I was introduced to someone by a business contact. We met to get to know each other. I immediately took a liking to the guy, and he asked for my help in getting new clients for his business. Within a week, I made a valuable introduction to him. He met with my contact, and soon thereafter they embarked on what could be a very lucrative business relationship. Guess what? Not a single thanks from the guy. I obviously didn't make the introduction to get a thank you, but not getting one was certainly downright annoying and, actually, quite disrespectful. It would be simple to call me, send me an email, or invite me out to celebrate and show his appreciation. But not a single word. Though I certainly do not hold a grudge, the guy's failure to say something so simple and respectful put my mind in a different place with that individual. I have many people I could help who are appreciative, and they get my attention and valuable resources, not the takers of the world who don't show common decency. Say thank you when you can. It will be remembered, and so will the failure to do so.

THE ZEN OF RULE 18

I'm proud of my kids for many reasons. But one of things I'm most proud of is how my wife and I always encouraged them to say thank you when appropriate. The best example I can think of is in a restaurant. We've always tried to get out to eat as a family as much as we could in light of everyone's busy schedules. When they were very young and a server would take their order or bring their beverage or food, they wouldn't think twice about simply digging in right away—without saying thank you. Servers have one of the toughest jobs, and they deserve our utmost respect (Rule 17). I remember back when my wife and I used to remind them: "Say thank you." At first, I doubt they even really appreciated the importance of thanking the server—too young. But over time, I noticed that they started to say it on their own. It brought a smile to my face when I listened to each of them say it. The most recent family meal to this writing was just this evening. We were in a restaurant, and each of them (now instinctively) said thank you to our server. And I watched the server's response each time. She smiled at each of them and said, "You're welcome." I smiled, too, as I watched because I knew they really wanted to say it and that they now realize how important it is to say those words. Look for opportunities everywhere to say thank you to people. It's the right thing to do and makes everyone involved feel good.

KEY TAKEAWAY

Thank and thank often.

Rule 19

Socially Reward Through Your Sincere Praise

*I think you need to love giving compliments
as much as you love receiving them.*

—Yami Gautam (Indian actress)

DO THIS!

Compliment people when they deserve it.

WHY?

Praise makes people feel good.[1] The social reward of a compliment can actually be as or more satisfying as a monetary reward.[2] In business, praise can create a better work environment and encourages employee creativity.[3] In a romantic relationship, compliments

---

[1] K. Izuma, D. N. Saito and N. Sadato, "Processing of Social and Monetary Rewards in the Human Striatum," *Neuron* 58, no. 2 (2008): 284–294, https://doi.org/10.1016/j.neuron.2008.03.020.

[2] Id.

[3] Jan Dul and Canan Ceylan, "Work Environments for Employee Creativity," *Ergonomics* 54, no. 1 (2011): 12-20, DOI: 10.1080/00140139.2010.542833.

between partners are primary ways of giving and receiving love.[4] No matter the situation, praise is important to fostering good feelings in any relationship. If both people sincerely compliment each other, then the social rewards that result are priceless.

Compliments help us to express our appreciation for others, and appreciation is fundamental to relationships. A compliment is "any sort of sincere appreciation of a trait in someone or a behavior or an appearance."[5] When we feel appreciated by someone, we feel more connected to that person.

A simple ratio to keep in mind as you develop relationships is this: your compliments should be five times the number of criticisms (if there are any criticisms). In a successful relationship, that 5-to-1 ratio of compliments to criticisms can indicate the likelihood of the growth of the relationship.[6] Pay attention to how much you praise someone, and be mindful of how much that person praises you. Do the same for criticisms. If you are not near the 5-to-1 ratio, look for sincere ways to increase your compliments of the other person.

A FEW TIPS ABOUT RULE 19

- Paying someone a compliment is a great way to break the ice. For example, if you've heard good things about someone and are just meeting that person for the first time, let that person

---

[4] Gary Chapman, *The 5 Love Languages: The Secret to Love that Lasts* (Chicago: Northfield Publishing; Reprint edition, 2014).

[5] Marcia Naomi Berger, *Marriage Meetings for Lasting Love: 30 Minutes a Week to the Relationship You've Always Wanted* Paperback (Novato: New World Library; 1st edition, 2014).

[6] Kyle Benson, "The Magic Relationship Ratio, According to Science," https://www.gottman.com/blog/the-magic-relationship-ratio-according-science/.

know you've heard many great things about that individual and are looking forward to getting to know him or her. Just think about how you'd feel if someone started a conversation with you like that.

- In a romantic relationship, the last thing you want to do is make someone feel uncomfortable by showering too many compliments before you get to know that person. As your familiarity increases, it becomes more appropriate to shower that person with more and more praise.

- If someone is successful at something, praise him or her for that success. Let that person know you're impressed with that achievement.

- When you receive a compliment, be humble when you say thank you (Rule 18). How we respond to compliments reveals part of our character. If we are boastful or unappreciative, people will be turned off and won't want to invest in the relationship.

- If possible, praise people in public. Nothing beats a sincere compliment more than when others can hear it, too. Of course, be careful not to embarrass someone. Public praise can be really effective in generating good feelings from the person getting the compliment.

TRAIN WRECK: WHEN RULE 19 DERAILS

Lack of appreciation can eat away at a relationship over time. One of my friends was working his way up the ladder in his company. Gifted with extraordinary sales skills and work ethic, he rose through the ranks over many years. He had many of the symbols of business success you'd expect, including a beautiful home, fancy cars, and expensive clothing. But one thing was missing: the appreciation of his colleagues. Maybe they were jealous of his success or felt inadequate compared to him—who knows? Since he is a humble guy, he never expected a compliment. But one day he thought long and hard about the fact that, except for the money he was making, no one had ever given him a meaningful pat on the back. The next day he decided to find a business home where people actually care about each other and recognize each other for their successes, giving everyone on the team the encouragement and respect (Rule 17) due as colleagues. Today he's with another company and, although no place is perfect, he's extremely happy, thriving well beyond his prior level of success. Failure to show appreciation with compliments or other signs of gratitude can end even the longest of relationships.

THE ZEN OF RULE 19

As a leader in my law firm, I have the pleasure of working with some of the best attorneys I've ever met during my decades in the profession. They are smart, incredibly knowledgeable, have unrivaled work ethic, and are loyal to the firm and each other. Any business leader will likely tell you that finding excellent people to work with is extremely difficult. We work on complicated matters for some of the best clients in the world, and our clients depend on us to perform at the highest level. Having such a great team is an honor, and I feel grateful every day. It's because of my sincere gratitude that I take every opportunity to compliment a job well done. Our job isn't easy. It's stressful much of the time, and there's a lot at stake. To complete a matter successfully is a great thing in any business, and that success should be noticed by leadership. I love to pick up the phone or email my colleagues and let them know I thought they did a great job and how much I appreciate them. I hope in some way that sharing my thoughts on their performance makes them feel good. Good feelings in the workplace are important (as they are in every relationship). Paying a compliment also makes me feel good. Make everyone feel good by identifying opportunities around you every day to pay people compliments they deserve.

KEY TAKEAWAY

Give people compliments they deserve.

Rule 20

Build Rapport and Reap Relationship Riches

Rapport is the ultimate tool for producing results with other people.
—Tony Robbins (American author, coach, speaker, and philanthropist)

DO THIS!

Build great rapport with people to more effectively communicate and establish trust.

WHY?

Rapport exists when people feel in sync or are on the same wavelength because they feel similar in some way. We prefer people whom we perceive to be like ourselves.[1] People feel connected when rapport exists between them. Both are focused on and interested in what the other person is saying or doing; both are friendly and happy

---

[1] Adrianna C. Jenkins, C. Neil Macrae and Jason P. Mitchell. "Repetition suppression of ventromedial prefrontal activity during judgments of self and others," Proceedings of the National Academy of Sciences 105, no. 11 (Mar 2008): 4507-4512, DOI: 10.1073/pnas.0708785105.

and share a common understanding of some sort.[2] Moreover, their energy levels, vocal tone, and body language are consistent.[3] Basically, people who have rapport click with each other. This "clicking" can happen right away when people first meet, or it can occur over time as the relationship develops.

Instead of leaving rapport to chance and hoping it miraculously occurs, actively try to build rapport during your conversations with people. Work to get people feeling similar to you in some way from the moment you meet them and as the relationship grows. There are many ways do this.

Small talk is a good way to begin building rapport. Polish anthropologist Bronisław Malinowski was the first person to study small talk, in 1923. He defined small talk as "purposeless expressions of preference or aversion, accounts of irrelevant happenings, [and] comments on what is perfectly obvious." [4] Basically, saying something for the sake of being sociable, as opposed to communicating information. Look for things you have in common, and talk about them for the sake of talking about them and being friendly. Topics like hometown sports, the weather, kids, vacations, music, and so forth can be good small-talk topics.

Neuro-Linguistic Programming (NLP) is also helpful in building rapport. NLP is an approach that educates people on how to communicate more effectively and build rapport. Although we tend to focus on the words in a conversation, only 7% of communication

---

[2] L. Tickle-Degnen and R. Rosenthal, "The Nature of Rapport and Its Nonverbal Correlates," *Psychological Inquiry* 1, no. 4 (1990): 285-293, Retrieved June 20, 2021, from http://www.jstor.org/stable/1449345.

[3] Id.

[4] http://s-f-walker.org.uk/pubsebooks/pdfs/ogden-richards-meaning-all.pdf.

occurs through words.[5] The balance of communication—93%—is nonverbal.[6]

Here are two ways to communicate nonverbally to establish rapport. First, mirror and match the other person's body language. Doing so will make people feel better about you.[7] If someone is sitting straight up, sit straight up. If the person's legs are crossed, cross your legs. If someone uses his or her hands a lot to make a point, use your hands to make a point. Second, match a person's voice patterns. People like voices that are similar to theirs.[8] Listen to how a person is speaking. Match the person's volume and pace. If the other person's tone is conversational, then match it. If the tone is excited, then match it. Again, try to match effectively to achieve a subconscious rapport.

A FEW TIPS ABOUT RULE 20

- Always be genuine when establishing rapport. For example, when you attempt to mirror and match someone, you don't want to be so obvious that it's recognized by the other person and considered insincere.

- Make a list of go-to small-talk topics. Make sure you're personally interested in them and that they would be easy topics to

[5] Albert Mehrabian, *Silent Messages* (Belmont, CA: Wadsworth, 1971).

[6] Id.

[7] S. Kühn, B. C. Müller, R. B. van Baaren, A. Wietzker, A. Dijksterhuis and M. Brass, "Why Do I Like You When You Behave Like Me? Neural Mechanisms Mediating Positive Consequences of Observing Someone Being Imitated." *Social Neuroscience* 5, no. 4 (2010): 384–392, https://doi.org/10.1080/17470911003633750.

[8] M. Babel, G. McGuire and J. King, "Towards a More Nuanced View of Vocal Attractiveness." *PLoS ONE* 9, no. 2 (2014): e88616. https://doi.org/10.1371/journal.pone.0088616.

bring up to most people you meet. Then convert those topics into questions for the other person in a conversation.

- Be attentive to the type of person someone is beyond his or her words. Train yourself to get to know that part of a person not disclosed through words alone. The more you get to know that inner person, the better you can naturally mirror and match that individual.

- Rapport can be created through shared experiences, like attending a sporting event, concert, conference, or party together. The memory of a shared experience that is rewarding to both people will have a lasting positive effect.

- If you sense that rapport you have previously built has been lost or is weakening, for whatever reason, remember that it can be re-established. All you need to do is recreate those things that brought you into rapport with the other person in the first place.

THE ZEN OF RULE 20

Many of my friends are leaders in business. They own or manage service firms, manufacturing companies, private equity firms, real estate development companies, and a host of other businesses. One of them related a haunting story to me about someone his firm hired in a junior position. The person worked in a private office and kept to himself for the most part. From day one, everyone else in the office noticed that the person was coming in late, dressed much less professionally than the others, didn't say hello when passing in the office, didn't smile, and didn't conform to a number of the firm's standard administrative protocols. During necessary work conversations, the person would appear uninterested and unengaged—quite the opposite of the others in the office who, for the most part, approached their jobs with enthusiasm as team players. Even in light of these circumstances, the firm continued to invest in the person since he was actually good at what he did. Then the great recession of 2008 hit, and the firm needed to lay off a portion of its workforce. My friend said the leaders of the firm got together to discuss whom would need to be let go, and there wasn't a single leader who spoke up to protect and argue for retaining that person. He had simply not established rapport in any sense of the word with anyone in the firm. Building rapport can add significant value to a relationship, while lack of rapport can make it much easier for people to end a relationship.

GETTING RULE 20 BACK ON TRACK

When I think about building rapport with people, the memories of a host of first-time meetings I've had over the years come to mind. I get introduced to new people all the time as a result of my legal business and my other business and personal endeavors. I love to meet new people. We are all different, and I enjoy learning about everyone and hearing their personal stories and figuring out how we can help each other. One of the things I like to do when I get introduced to someone is get out with them over a meal or coffee. We are most always sitting right across from each other. From the moment we sit down, I start to get a sense as to their inner person, not because I'm analyzing someone, but because I want to be sensitive to not doing or saying something that will throw us out of a rapport-building moment. I try to mirror and match and bring up timely and interesting small-talk topics to make the person as comfortable as possible. In the age of video conferencing, I have had to try to replicate my in-person rapport-building efforts by way of video. It's definitely not the same as sitting right across from someone, but the basic concepts of NLP and small talk and getting to know someone's inner person are still relevant. Practice building rapport every chance you get, whether in person or by phone or video and even by email. The skills for building rapport cross over all mediums of communication.

KEY TAKEAWAY

Intentionally work to establish rapport with others.

Rule 21

Gift Positivity for Positive Results

The most worthwhile thing is to try to put happiness into the lives of others.

—Robert Baden-Powell (British General)

DO THIS!

Maintain a positive outlook on life, and bring your happiness into your relationships.

WHY?

Studies have demonstrated the many benefits of living a happier, more fulfilling life. Happier people are rewarded with greater social rewards and interactions; they have more energy and activity, a higher level of self-control and ability to cope, a more resilient immune system, increased longevity,[1] greater personal confidence, self-esteem, and control; and they have more optimism, increased likeability, energy, physical well-being, and

---

[1] Sonja Lyubomirsky, Kennon Sheldon and David Schkade, "Pursuing Happiness: The Architecture of Sustainable Change," *Review of General Psychology* 9, no. 2 (2005): 111–131.

creativity.[2] For all of these reasons, it's smart to seriously consider the concept of happiness every day as we build relationships.

Injecting "positive affect"—essentially, happiness—into a relationship increases the likelihood of making that relationship a success.[3] If the other person perceives you as being a happy person, the relationship will be more pleasant, there will be more of a connection, and each person will tend to be more supportive of the other.[4]And the relationship has a greater chance of being long-lasting.[5]

To reap the benefits of happiness as a relationship-builder, you need to always be mindful of your own happiness level and work to stay positive in light of negative things in your life. If you can reach an adequate level of happiness, then you bring your positivity into your relationships. Let others know you're happy by your positive choices and words, attitude, and cooperative nature. Being and remaining happy is difficult with the pressures and uncertainties of life, but there are ways to practice happiness every day to stay positive as much as possible. For example, exercise more,[6] simply think

---

[2] Sonja Lyubomirsky, Laura King and Ed Diener, "The Benefits of Frequent Positive Affect: Does Happiness Lead to Success?" *Psychological Bulletin* 131, no. 6 (2005): 803–855.

[3] S. M. Moore, E. Diener and K. Tan, "Using multiple methods to more fully understand causal relations: Positive affect enhances social relationships," In E. Diener, S. Oishi and L. Tay (eds.), *Handbook of Well-being*, (Salt Lake City, UT: DEF Publishers, 2018), DOI:nobascholar.com

[4] Id.

[5] Id.

[6] George Mammen and Guy Faulkner, "Physical Activity and the Prevention of Depression: A Systematic Review of Prospective Studies," *American Journal of Preventive Medicine* 45, iss. 5 (2013): 649-657, ISSN 0749-3797, https://doi.org/10.1016/j.amepre.2013.08.001.

positive thoughts,[7] and consciously focus on and write down your blessings—what you are grateful for.[8] On the flip side, write down your negative thoughts and literally throw them in the garbage,[9] and focus on your strengths as opposed to your weaknesses.[10] These are just a few ways to give yourself the gift of happiness so you can enter your relationships armed with positivity to maximize the likelihood of relationship success.

A FEW TIPS ABOUT RULE 21

- Think about when you meet people who seem happy. What are their characteristics? Do they smile (Rule 3)? Use positive language? Have a zest for life? Reflect the characteristics of other happy people you meet.

- Strive for an "enduring level of happiness" by engaging in "activities [you] very much like doing," which will help you achieve "authentic happiness," the most potent type of happiness.[11]

---

[7] Shawn Achor, *The Happiness Advantage: The Seven Principles of Positive Psychology That Fuel Success and Performance at Work* (New York: Crown Business, 2010).

[8] R. A. Emmons and M. E. McCullough, "Counting Blessings Versus Burdens: An Experimental Investigation of Gratitude and Subjective Well-being in Daily Life," *Journal of Personality and Social Psychology* 84, no. 2 (2003): 377–389. https://doi.org/10.1037//0022-3514.84.2.377.

[9] P. Briñol, M. Gascó, R. E. Petty and J. Horcajo, "Treating Thoughts as Material Objects Can Increase or Decrease Their Impact on Evaluation," *Psychological Science* 24, no. 1 (2013): 41–47, https://doi.org/10.1177/0956797612449176.

[10] Tayyab Rashid and Afroze Anjum, "340 Ways to Use VIA Character Strengths," https://www.actionforhappiness.org/media/52486/340_ways_to_use_character_strengths.pdf.

[11] Martin Seligman, *Authentic Happiness: Using the New Positive Psychology to Realize Your Potential for Lasting Fulfillment* (New York: Free Press, 2002).

- Remain upbeat and positive during a conversation. No matter the topic, look for ways to put a positive spin on it and bring up the emotional tone of the conversation. People want to be uplifted, not be brought down by negativity.

- Be mindful that not everyone may be as happy as you for any number of reasons. Avoid making someone feel worse by coming on as too happy. That said, look for ways to cheer that person up, and direct the conversation into a more positive direction.

- When you're in a funk (we all are from time to time), it's okay to tell someone you're feeling down or not in the best of moods. It's better to be honest about how you feel than to allow the other person to misinterpret how you feel as somehow his or her fault.

THE ZEN OF RULE 21

Back in 2014, I authored a book on the topic of happiness, titled *happy is cool: how to ignite the true happiness in you.* I wrote the book for my kids. I wanted to leave them something to help them be happy for the rest of their lives. A lofty goal, I know, but one worth pursuing. We were at a water park in Lake Geneva, Wisconsin, when all four of my kids were much younger, and they were splashing in the water, smiling ear to ear, having the time of their lives—happy as can be. Then I got an overwhelming feeling: I wanted to write down whatever I could to keep them happy like that forever. I started writing that moment and ended up with thirty ideas that over the next number of months evolved into a full-length book that everyone of all ages would, I believe, find helpful. I'm proud of that book and even prouder of my kids for the great young adults they have become. My primary hope for them is that they're happy and enjoy the very best relationships as they make their journey through life. That, too, is my hope for you. Be happy! Be cool!

KEY TAKEAWAY

Stay positive, and bring your positivity into your relationships.

Conclusion

MY HOPE IN THIS book is that the *21 Rules* can be an inspiring way for you to start building better connections with others in your life. A big part of life is appreciating the blessings we have and the opportunities in front of us. Building a unique relationship with someone is one of the most awesome experiences we can have. Remember, we all want a connection with others. The skills to build the very best relationships can provide you all that you desire in life and business.

Rules are important. They're explicit principles that govern an activity. In this book, the activity is building unique connections with other people—the essence of starting and growing relationships. The idea in these pages is not to provide a be-all, end-all list of ways you can build relationships. My hope is that you can use these principles as guideposts to measure your progress as you build better and more unique relationships.

Like most rules, there are exceptions. The *21 Rules* are subject to your personal style and comfort level. Not every rule will apply to you or be something you need to improve upon. There are likely rules that you've already mastered and maybe others you can focus on more consciously. Even with principles that might seem self-evident to you, understanding the scientific research underlying these principles can help you put them in better perspective in your life and business—and perhaps give you added motivation to use them more intentionally every day in every interaction you have with people.

Most, if not all, of the *21 Rules* are simple to master. Some might require more practice for some people compared to others, simply based on different personality types and past experience building relationships. But no matter your current level of confidence in growing your business and life relationships, if you are mindful of the *21 Rules*, they will become second nature. The details of each rule are important, but it's the general idea that counts the most. Start incorporating bits and pieces of the rules you find most useful to you in your day-to-day life. It could be one rule or two rules. It doesn't matter as long as you start somewhere to gain greater depth in your relationship-building skills. As the depth of your skills with people increases, so will your confidence in bringing more and more rules strategically into your relationships.

Come back to these rules often, as a reminder of the substance of the rules themselves and their key takeaway ideas, as well as the science behind the rules. If the science is top of mind as you continue to practice the *21 Rules*, you will get more out of them, because you will use them more confidently knowing exactly the practical effect they will have in any relationship. These rules are tools, and tools are meant to be used to make jobs and other activities easier and more efficient. Make developing relationships easier by using these rules. Increase the efficiency and speed with which you get close to people and maintain those connections for the long term.

Practice every day. Like a great musician who always wants to get better, you need to practice. You can start now by working through the exercises that follow. As you gain greater experience practicing the *21 Rules*, you will gain greater and greater depth with them and the effect of the rules will become more powerful. You have the ability to connect with just about anyone you meet. Once you connect with people, both you and others can live richer and more fulfilling lives. Each person can achieve his or her goals and satisfy the basic human need of really connecting with other people.

Use the *21 Rules* to master the art and science of relationships in life and business and hit it off with people!

Hit It Off Rule 1 Exercise

Take a Fresh Look at Eye Contact to Convey Emotion

Establish and maintain an appropriate level of eye contact during your conversations with others.

Science shows that eye contact is a key element that connects humans during social communication.

Use this exercise to strategize on how you can best harness the power of eye contact from the moment you meet someone and as you continue to develop your relationship with that person.

1. Always be socially appropriate when maintaining eye contact. Be mindful not to maintain too much eye contact. Next time you are in a conversation with someone, note the amount of eye contact each of you has during the conversation. Particularly, note how and when each of you breaks eye contact. Write down 3 ways to break eye contact and where you could look, in each case without coming off as rude or disinterested (e.g., looking down at your food while eating or your glass as you raise it).

_____

_____

_____

_____

_____

2. The power of eye contact is much less effective if other aspects of communication are distracting. Are you speaking too loudly or softly; too fast or slow? Slumping in your chair or standing too close? Write down 3 things you should be aware of in a conversation with someone to avoid distractions from the power of good eye contact (e.g., being aware of the cadence of the other person's speech so you can match it and not come off as uncomfortably different in how quickly you speak to the other person).

_____

_____

_____

_____

_____

3. You benefit if people recognize your empathy for them through your eyes. Convey your empathy for someone by listening to and learning about that person. Write down 3 ways you can use your eyes to convey your empathy for someone (e.g., by staying focused on their eyes and NOT breaking eye contact if they are telling you something very important/sensitive).

_____

_____

_____

_____

_____

4. Combine a smile (Rule 3) with eye contact when appropriate. Write down 3 ways you can try to convey your joy about your interaction with someone through a genuine smile (e.g., starting to form

a smile on your face when someone is describing something that is exciting), and note the level/degree of eye contact while you're doing so.

_____

_____

_____

_____

_____

5. People can tell from our eyes in many cases if we are happy or sad, excited or fearful, angry or surprised, etc. Our eyes convey our inner person and are powerful parts of our personhood. Write down 3 sentences, one each that conveys a different emotion (e.g., happiness, sadness, excitement, fear, anger, surprise). Then say them aloud to someone (who agrees to allow you to practice on them) and pay attention to whether you squint your eyes, open them, keep them stoic as you speak, etc. Then ask the other person to describe how your eyes added to the effect of the particular sentence/emotion.

_____

_____

_____

_____

_____

Hit It Off Rule 2 Exercise

Prepare to Achieve Goals Efficiently—In Reverse

Imagine yourself as if you've already accomplished a goal for a relationship, and then plan backwards thinking about all the steps that you had to take to get to that goal.

Science shows that "future retrospection" (essentially planning goal achievement in reverse) increases our productivity, motivation, and confidence, and reduces stress as we pursue our goals.

Use this exercise to practice what might seem counter-intuitive—starting with the goal for a relationship in mind first and working backwards to make your pursuit of that goal as efficient as possible.

1. Think about 3 relationships you have right now and write down an end goal for each relationship. In doing so, think through why you are in each relationship to begin with, and the very best desired result of your relationship (e.g., a personal goal might be getting married to your significant other; in business, a goal might be to get the sale).

_____

_____

_____

_____

_____

2. For each of the goals you wrote down in No. 1 above, write down what you would say to the other person in each relationship to discuss the idea of agreeing on that goal and encouraging the other person to buy into the process of working toward that goal together (e.g., if you are an author, and would like to collaborate with another author on an article, you might say something like this to the other author: "We should consider co-writing an article as it would help both of us to reach an even larger audience to share our common thoughts on a particular topic. What do you think?").

_____

_____

_____

_____

_____

3. Assume that each person you approached about a common goal above is not terribly excited about your idea. You can either redirect your energy to another person who has a similar goal or simply modify the initial goal to one that will still be rewarding to you. Write down a revision to each goal in an attempt to better encourage the other person to buy-in (e.g., "Instead of an article, how about we do a joint speaking event?").

_____

_____

_____

_____

_____

4. Now think backwards for each goal, and write down a list of things you would do to achieve each goal, starting with goal achievement, a week before, month before, six months before, etc. Consider the details (e.g., when thinking about an important dinner with someone, determine the restaurant, other guests, something to do after dinner, etc.).

_____

_____

_____

_____

_____

5. Now that you've mapped out the steps to achieve your goal—in reverse—think about what might happen along the way that could require you to change certain steps. You always want to be alert to possible setbacks and be prepared up front to address them efficiently as they occur. For example, if you plan on co-writing an article on a particular topic and before publication someone writes a similar article (certainly possible), you might need to have a few other related topics handy so you can reboot the collaboration quickly.

_____

_____

_____

_____

_____

Hit It Off Rule 3 Exercise

Remember That a Simple Smile Is Tied to Deep Trust

**Use a genuine smile to really help you strike up
a new relationship with someone.**

**Science shows that increased smile intensity is associated
with greater trustworthiness.**

*Use this exercise to think through how you can use the power of a genuine
smile to elicit feelings of trust and loyalty in your relationships.*

1. Next time you speak with someone, observe how much or how
little that person smiles while you are talking. Are the smiles tied to
humor or happy moments in the discussion? Does the other person
use a smile to drive a point home? Does the person not smile at all,
and can you guess why they cannot bring themselves to smile (e.g.,
are they nervous or sad?). Do this with 3 people and write down
your observations.

_____

_____

_____

_____

_____

2. Sincere smiles are welcomed. Insincere or patronizing smiles are not. Write down 3 situations where a smile made during a conversation would be considered genuine.

_____

_____

_____

_____

_____

3. Next time you meet someone for the first time, look in the other person's eyes and share a genuine smile with that person. Do this when asking someone for something such as ordering food in a restaurant or asking someone at a table to pass the salt and pepper. Also try this when proposing an idea to someone. Do this a few times and write down your observations. Do you feel that the reaction you got from the other person was influenced by the fact that you looked them in the eyes and smiled?

_____

_____

_____

_____

_____

4. Remember to smile back at someone if that person smiles at you. But do so appropriately with an equal amount of enthusiasm. Think about 3 times when someone might smile at you, and write down how you would respond, including the degree of a smile you would share back with that person, and something you would say to enrich

the situation (e.g., if someone enters an elevator and smiles at you, you can say, "Hi! How's it going?" as you smile back).

_____

_____

_____

_____

_____

5. Assume you are in a conversation with someone, and a smile is not warranted. Write down 3 other ways to use your facial features to show positivity which can be helpful in building a relationship (e.g., keeping the sides of your mouth pitched slightly upward and gently nodding as the other person is speaking will demonstrate a sense of interest and engagement).

_____

_____

_____

_____

_____

Hit It Off Rule 4 Exercise

Consciously Listen
to Build Acceptance

Practice active listening—consciously listen to the other person during a conversation so you can hear the complete message of that individual.

Science shows that human connection is more likely if we are actively listening to someone because by doing so we demonstrate unconditional acceptance and unbiased reflection.

Use this exercise to develop your active listening skills and increase the likelihood of understanding what someone is really trying to say, thus fostering feelings of acceptance and trust in the other person.

1. Pay attention to your next 3 conversations with people. Are you staying focused on the other person and what he or she is saying. Are you thinking about what to say most of the time someone is speaking? Do you find yourself thinking about a pre-determined goal or outcome for that conversation? Do you find yourself getting distracted by side conversations around you? Write down your observations from these conversations.

_____

_____

_____

_____

2. Think about a recent conversation you had someone. Write down 3 things about that person that might have given you a clue as to the true meaning of what he or she told you (e.g., the person's personality, demeanor, tone of voice, body movements, line of work).

_____

_____

_____

_____

_____

3. In your next 3 conversations, remember to ask questions to clarify the intent of the other person to demonstrate that you really heard what was said, and, more importantly, that you're interested in it. After clarifying what the person meant, write down similarities and distinctions between what was said and how you initially interpreted those words.

_____

_____

_____

_____

_____

4. Practice summarizing someone's comments by writing down 3 things someone might tell you during a conversation, and then follow-up by writing how you might go about summarizing what that person said in a respectful and seamless way (e.g., If someone says, "Whenever my adult kid asks me for advice when they do something

wrong, I find myself remembering all the things I did wrong growing up, so I never feel comfortable giving my own kid advice on how to avoid the same mistake in the future," you might say, "So, if I understand you, you're not feeling confident in giving advice because you weren't perfect growing up, but you would love to figure out a way to get out of your own way and provide the necessary advice and help your kid.")

_____

_____

_____

_____

_____

5. If you properly practice active listening by staying focused on what the other person is saying and placing yourself in their shoes to discern that person's true intent, you will sometimes be tempted to react with your own strong opinions that might be contrary to what you've just heard. But any response needs to be respectful (Rule 17). Write down 3 things someone might say with which you disagree, and then follow-up with a response that is respectful (e.g., Someone might say, "I think God does or does not exist" (with which you disagree), and you might respond by saying, "That's such an interesting topic that great philosophers have been debating the existence of God since the beginning of time").

_____

_____

_____

_____

_____

Hit It Off Rule 5 Exercise

Share Personal Experiences to Create Relationship Depth

Learn about people through the mutual sharing of personal life experiences—a process called mutual self-disclosure.

Science shows that when people share personal details about themselves, such as their feelings, thoughts, and memories, they are more likely to build a deep and trusting relationship.

Use this exercise to strategize on how you can better learn about other people from the moment you meet them and as you continue to develop your relationships.

1. When you first meet someone—that very first encounter—you want to put them at ease with you. What simple statements can you make when you first meet someone to put them at ease and give that person the opportunity to take control of the conversation for a while? (e.g., "Tell me a little bit about yourself.") Write down 3 simple, icebreaking statements you can have at your disposal when you first meet someone.

_____

_____

_____

_____

_____

2. It's typically a good idea for you to begin the process of mutual self-disclosure. One easy way to do this is to share information about your family. This can be a great way to get the other person to talk about his or her family, a comfortable topic for many people. What are you comfortable sharing about your family with someone you meet for the first time? Write down 3 details about your family you are willing to share.

_____

_____

_____

_____

_____

3. Speaking of details about yourself, sharing a personal detail about yourself that few people know can be a powerful way to create a bond with someone. But never share a detail about yourself unless you are 100% comfortable doing so. What is something about yourself that few people know that you'd feel comfortable sharing with someone? Can you think of 3 things?

_____

_____

_____

_____

_____

4. Asking open-ended questions earlier in a relationship makes people feel most comfortable as you get to know them. Use more direct questions about the person after getting to know him or her more. Once people feel more comfortable with you, they will be

more willing to share specific personal information. Can you think of 3 open-ended questions (e.g., "What type of music do you like?") you could ask someone early in a relationship?

_____

_____

_____

_____

_____

5. If someone shares something that is difficult for that person to say (e.g., how they made a mistake), then consider sharing something similar. This will put the person in a more comfortable position about what they told you and will now consider you a closer friend for it. What are 3 things that are difficult for you to share but would be willing to share to create a closer bond with someone?

_____

_____

_____

_____

_____

Hit It Off Rule 6 Exercise

Build Connection Through Trust

Building mutual trust with others is an important relationship-building skill.

Relationship expert, John Gottman, concludes that "trust is essential to healthy relationships."

Use this exercise to be more intentional in building trust with people as you develop a relationship with them.

1. Have a good reason to trust others. Make sure the other person's values align with yours. Without aligned values, trusting someone else can be riskier than normal. Think about your governing values. What things are important to you and write down the top 3 values you have which you can keep top of mind as you evaluate the likelihood of someone trusting you, and which values you can try to identify in someone else to give you more confidence that he or she is the type of person with whom you can, in turn, place your trust.

_____

_____

_____

_____

_____

2. You can instill trust in others if you give them a reason to trust you, including sharing stories about how you've proven your trust to others in the past. People are going to be more trusting if they know you have a track record for being honest and trustworthy. Write down 3 times when people have trusted you to do something, and you came through for them. Try to pick times that were particularly challenging to emphasize your trustworthiness even when it's difficult to do something people are trusting you to do.

_____

_____

_____

_____

_____

3. Think about times when people have told you that they were let down by someone. Write down 3 of those things, and then follow-up by explaining how you would have avoided letting those people down. How would you have acted differently and why?

_____

_____

_____

_____

_____

4. Sharing details about when you were let down by someone and how that affected you can convey to another person how sensitive you are about NOT letting others down. Think about times when

people have let you down—when they proved themselves untrust-worthy. Then follow-up with how those situations made you feel.

_____

_____

_____

_____

_____

5. We all make mistakes. We're far from perfect. Write down 3 times when you let someone down—when you could have been more reliable, even when you did not intend on letting them down. Then follow-up with how you felt. And remember to give a heartfelt apology whenever you fall short in the future.

_____

_____

_____

_____

_____

Hit It Off Rule 7 Exercise

Provide Value
to Promote Gratitude

**Providing some sort of value to people strengthens relationships
and contributes to relationship connection and satisfaction.**

**Science shows that the experience of gratitude inspires others
who have benefited from acts of kindness to repay their benefactors.**

*Use this exercise to build your value network and maximize the feelings of
gratitude in others.*

1. Write down 3 things you can provide to others that would be
considered valuable (e.g., providing access to needed information or
a business connection, making an introduction to someone they've
wanted to meet, being a trusted friend and someone to do things with).

_____

_____

_____

_____

_____

2. Be assertive in asking people how you can help them. Let them
know you just want to be helpful as they pursue their goals in life and
business. Write down 3 ways to ask people how you can help them

(e.g., "What is your biggest obstacle in maximizing your business profits, because I might have someone in my network who can help you overcome that obstacle?)

_____

_____

_____

_____

_____

3. Be creative as you think about providing value. Think about 3 people you know and, in each case, their biggest potential "ask" of you. Write down a creative way to provide value to each person in a way that would satisfy their "ask."

_____

_____

_____

_____

_____

4. Always be growing your value network in business and life generally. Write down 3 ways you can continue to meet new and interesting people who are in positions of influence.

_____

_____

_____

_____

_____

5. Oftentimes, when you provide value to one person, you need to ask another person for a favor to help the first person. Make a list of 3 people you know today who you can ask for such a favor and the value they can provide to others in your network.

_____

_____

_____

_____

_____

Hit It Off Rule 8 Exercise

Use Humor to Convey
a Similar World View

**Weaving humor tastefully into your conversations with people
can increase your personal and business success.**

**Science shows that shared laughter is tied to relationship satisfaction
and can communicate to others that we have a similar worldview,
which strengthens our relationships.**

*Use this exercise to employ humor to boost your connections with others and
build fun and mutually enriching relationships.*

1. Make sure your humor is always tasteful. Never use inappropriate
humor. Create a list of hands-off topics—topics you will never weave
into your attempt to be humorous in a conversation. What are your
top 3 topics? Write them down.

_____

_____

_____

_____

_____

2. Stay away from telling canned jokes unless you're a professional comedian. That said, are there a few canned jokes you've used

to great success in the past? Can you think of 3? Write them down. If you cannot think of any, do not try to write your own jokes, unless you have aspirations of becoming a professional comedian, and then test them out on an open mic night at the local comedy club.

_____

_____

_____

_____

_____

3. Think about funny things in your life (e.g., your dog likes to carry its own leash on a walk, your cat meows your name (or at least it sounds like it), your co-worker (who you don't know that well) keeps calling you by another name no matter how many times you correct that person). Try to incorporate these humorous things into conversations when appropriate to lighten the mood. Write down 3 funny things in your life right now.

_____

_____

_____

_____

_____

4. Look for cues to be humorous. Spontaneity is much better than canned jokes. Pay attention to your future conversations and times when you could add a quip that is humorous. In preparation, can you think of 3 times during recent conversations when someone said

something that easily could have lent itself to a humorous comment in response? Write them down.

_____

_____

_____

_____

_____

5. It's one thing for you to weave tasteful humor into a conversation. And then there is how you respond when someone else does so. How will you respond? Laughing too much will be considered condescending. Laughing at an insensitive or otherwise inappropriate joke or statement can lead the other person to think less of you (even though the other person made the original statement). Think of ways you can respond to someone's humor that would be considered appropriate in light of the particular type of joke. Consider both appropriate and inappropriate humorous statements. Write down 3 ways to respond (e.g., a soft smile, wide smile, laughter, side-splitting laugher, no response).

_____

_____

_____

_____

_____

Hit It Off Rule 9 Exercise

Identify Shared Interests to Emphasize Like-Mindedness

Shared interests of any kind can establish and enhance relationships.

Science shows that sharing *rare* interests are highly effective in connecting people and enhancing interpersonal attraction.

Use this exercise to harness the power of sharing interests in a relationship and deepening the connection with others.

1. Think about what you really enjoy doing that you are truly passionate about and have a strong interest in. These are the things that you will want to incorporate into your relationships with others, as people will be most enthused by what you are passionate about. Write down 3 things you truly enjoy doing that you feel others might also enjoy.

_____

_____

_____

_____

_____

2. Time the invitation into your passion or hobby appropriately. Think about the things you wrote down in No. 1 above and consider when you might have an opening in a conversation to introduce your interest into it. What openings might a person give you to when it would be most appropriate to welcome someone into your world?

_____

_____

_____

_____

_____

3. Remember that not everyone will be receptive to your personal passions or hobbies. Imagine trying to bring someone into your world—into something that truly moves you and he or she is not into it. How do you respond? What do you say? Where do you go from there? Write down 3 ways to move forward in a seamless way.

_____

_____

_____

_____

_____

4. Hobbies are great ways to invite others to share in your world. Write down 3 hobbies you have. Many people only have one or two, so if you only have one or two, only write those down. No need to create another hobby if you already have at least one with which you are passionate. If you don't have any hobbies, think about what you

enjoy doing and start a hobby around it. For example, if you enjoy driving, join a car club.

_____

_____

_____

_____

_____

5. Another way to get the maximum benefit of Rule 9 is to express a sincere interest in the other person's passions and hobbies. Think of 3 people with whom you are trying to deepen your relationship. Do you know what their passions and/or hobbies are? Write them down. If you don't, consider how you can ask them what they are passionate about in life.

_____

_____

_____

_____

_____

Hit It Off Rule 10 Exercise

Harness Emotional Intelligence to Effectively Navigate Social Interactions

Emotional intelligence—the ability to perceive, appraise, and express emotions accurately and adaptively—increases your potential to have better relationships.

Science shows that people with higher emotional intelligence were found to have a higher likelihood for close and affectionate relationships.

Use this exercise to improve your emotional intelligence, which will ultimately increase the strength of your relationships.

1. Do this with the next 3 people to speak with in person: Be mindful of how you feel about what you're saying and observe how the other person is reacting to you. Then write down your observations.

_____

_____

_____

_____

2. Remember back to when someone said something that stirred you up—got you a little upset or frustrated. How did you respond? Did you react how many people react (i.e., with a purely knee-jerk emotional reaction)? Write down 3 examples of those interactions and note how you felt, particularly why you thought you had to respond the way you did. Then pay attention going forward and take a step back—and think more calmly and in a measured way that keeps the long-term relationship in mind—before responding in similar situations.

_____

_____

_____

_____

_____

3. When someone is speaking to you, are you truly listening to them in a way that will allow you to empathize with that person and measure your emotions? Try this for the next 3 conversations you have: Really try hard to practice your active listening skills (Rule 4) and see how that affects your ability to put yourself in the other person's shoes to measure his or her emotions. Then observe how that process affects your ability to communicate more effectively. Write down your observations.

_____

_____

_____

_____

_____

4. When faced with negativity in a conversation, do you ever take a break and come back to the situation refreshed and with a positive attitude? Try this the next 3 times you are confronted with this situation. Then write down your observations.

_____

_____

_____

_____

_____

5. Always remember to use your leadership skills to guide you in a conversation. Leaders focus on navigating a conversation in a productive way, avoiding distractions around unnecessary disagreements (Rule 14) and strategically handling polarizing topics (Rule 15). Can you remember 3 times when you got into a disagreement with someone or were faced with a polarizing topic in a conversation that made you feel uncomfortable? How would you modify your reaction to redirect the conversation in a way to accomplish your goals and help the other person accomplish his or her goals? Write down your thoughts.

_____

_____

_____

_____

_____

Hit It Off Rule 11 Exercise

Admit Mistakes and Earn Trust and Respect

Be mindful of the power of admitting your mistakes.

Science shows that admitting our mistakes fosters trust and cooperation in a relationship.

Use this exercise to harness the power of admitting your mistakes so people will find you more trustworthy and have more respect for you.

1. Never hesitate to admit your mistakes right away. Doing so is not easy and can lead to embarrassment. But not doing so can lead to an irreparable perception in the other person's mind that you are not trustworthy and tried to hide something. Can you think of 3 times when you choose not to admit a mistake and either ignore it or come up with an excuse to defend yourself? Write down your experiences and how you felt afterwards.

_____

_____

_____

_____

_____

2. When you make a mistake, you need to do your best to make things right. Can you remember 3 times when you made a mistake and did not try hard enough to make things right with the other person? Write down what you could have done differently if given a second chance.

_____

_____

_____

_____

_____

3. What type of apology do you give people when you make a mistake? Is your apology heartfelt? Think of 3 times when people made a mistake that hurt you in some way. How did you feel? Did the other person in each case apologize? Was it heartfelt? If so, how did that make you feel? If not, how did that make you feel? Write down your answers.

_____

_____

_____

_____

_____

4. Think of the 3 biggest mistakes you've ever made in your life. If you could have avoided those mistakes (which is the case most often), what could you have done differently to have avoided making those mistakes?

_____

_____

_____

_____

5. Think back to 3 times when people made mistakes that negatively affected you—and apologized for those mistakes. Did you accept their apologies? If so, why? If not, why? If you accepted an apology, did you pay attention to how that made the other person feel? Write down your recollections.

_____

_____

_____

_____

_____

Hit It Off Rule 12 Exercise

Be Confident, Be Compelling

**A confident person is perceived as competent, driven,
and kind—qualities we want in a partner,
whether in our personal lives or in business.**

**Science shows that confidence quickly and efficiently conveys
a perception of our value to others.**

*Use this exercise to massively increase the confidence that is within you so
as to maximize the likelihood that others will perceive you as competent,
driven, and kind.*

1. Pick 3 healthy and enjoyable relationships who currently have,
whether in business or life generally. Why do you feel they have been
successful? Write down the reasons why and keep them top of mind
as you develop additional, similar relationships in the future—this
will help fuel your confidence that you can do it again.

_____

_____

_____

_____

_____

2. Are there people with whom you are developing a new relationship now who would benefit from knowing the past relationship successes you noted in No. 1 above? If so, write down their names next to the applicable success and next time you speak with those people, share your stories with them. This will give others comfort that they can have that type of relationship with you as well.

_____

_____

_____

_____

_____

3. Be careful not to be too overconfident. That said, slight overconfidence can be very helpful in conveying your confidence to others, but never come off as arrogant. Do you know people who come off as arrogant? How do you feel when they do so? Have you ever been too overconfident, and why? Write down your thoughts.

_____

_____

_____

_____

_____

4. Can you remember 3 times in the past when you have not been as confident as you wish you had been? Do you remember why you couldn't muster the confidence required at the time? Write down

what, in each case, you could have done differently to be more confident in those situations.

_____

_____

_____

_____

_____

5. Think about and create 3 mantras you can say to yourself in any situation where you need to be as confident as possible (e.g., "I've done this a million times; now one more;" "I can do this"). Command yourself to confidence by writing down these mantras and remember to use them in situations where you need to draw on the confidence you know is within you.

_____

_____

_____

_____

_____

Hit It Off Rule 13 Exercise

Care Through Your Actions

Taking action is critical to the concept of caring.

Science shows that when a person perceives that you care about him or her, your relationship with that individual is enhanced because it serves as a protector and a buffer to stress for that person.

Use this exercise to be more mindful of the actions you can take that reflect how much you care about someone, which, in turn, will foster the relationship in a deep and meaningful way.

1. Make sure people know you're there for them. When you actually say something like: "I'm here for you—however I can help," people will not only appreciate your concern, but it sets the stage to ask questions about the situation and formulate actions you can take to help them. What other things can you say that conveys your care and concern for others? Write down 3 of them.

_____

_____

_____

_____

2. Remember to come up with strategic ways you can help another person who needs it. Assume someone has had a death in the family, what actions can you take (not just consoling words) to show how much you care? Write down 3 of those actions.

---

3. Caring involves a continuous emotional investment in someone's well-being. Think about someone with whom you have a current relationship and think about 3 ways to continually show you care. Write them down.

---

4. Utilize your value network (Rule 7) to take action to show you care. Think about people in your personal or business network who you could ask for a favor to help other people to show you care. Write down 3 of those people and what you think they can provide to someone else if asked.

---

5. Doing too much too soon or not enough (when you should do more) to help someone can be damaging to the relationship. Can you think of 3 actions you might take in a new relationship that might be considered "too soon" to do? Write them down.

_____

_____

_____

_____

_____

Hit It Off Rule 14 Exercise

If You Disagree, Search for Common Ground

**Work hard to maintain harmony
in your communications with people.**

**Your understanding of "the illusion of explanatory depth"
can help you to strategically navigate areas of potential disagreement.**

Use this exercise to be appeal to broader values of a person as opposed to the specific issue around which there is potential disagreement to diffuse the situation and get both people focused on areas of agreement.

1. We tend to want to defend ourselves if someone disagrees with us, or to inject our own contrary opinions when someone says something with which we disagree. But we need to avoid the temptation to prove ourselves right all the time. Think about a few occasions when you pushed back when someone said something with which you disagreed. Write down 3 feelings or thoughts you had when you found yourself pushing back, and then write down ways you could have responded instead to preserve harmony in the conversation.

_____

_____

_____

_____

_____

202 | HIT IT OFF

2. We're all victim to the illusion of explanatory depth (i.e., we confuse a shallow familiarity with general concepts for real, in-depth knowledge). Unless we're an expert in an area of knowledge, we could very well be relying on a weak position on a topic if we persist in arguing our case. This mistake can encourage the other person to dig in and commit to fighting. Think about topics you've found yourself arguing about in the recent past. Be honest with yourself and write down 3 such topics and rate the depth of your knowledge of each topic from 1 to 10, with 10 being the knowledge of an expert. Notice any patterns?

_____

_____

_____

_____

_____

3. Assume you find yourself in a conversation and cannot avoid an argument. There obviously will be such situations notwithstanding your attempt to avoid a vocal—perhaps tense—disagreement. Write down 3 things you can say to the other person to show that person respect for his or her position even though you vehemently disagree with what you're hearing.

_____

_____

_____

_____

_____

4. Agree when you can. Avoid saying things like, "No, I don't think so," or "I think you're wrong." Write down 3 statements someone might say to you with which you disagree. Then write down something about each statement with which you can creatively agree.

_____

_____

_____

_____

_____

5. Remember to remain calm, empathic, and respectful of the other person if you disagree. Always avoid unnecessary negativity. For each statement you wrote down in No. 4 above, how might you be able to completely redirect the conversation calmly to move on to another topic and avoid further disagreement? Write down your answers.

_____

_____

_____

_____

_____

Hit It Off Rule 15 Exercise

Be Strategic About Polarizing Topics

When you first meet someone, avoid sensitive topics that might be emotional triggers for that person.

Stick to topics that are universally accepted as non-confrontational.

Use this exercise to improve your ability to avoid tough topics when you first meet someone, and strategically respond to a polarizing topic that person might bring up during a conversation.

1. Some people will bring up polarizing topics during small talk. Try to look for ways to redirect the conversation away from those topics to other topics that are less confrontational. But do so in a respectful way. Can you think of 3 ways to redirect a conversation away from a confrontational topic to one that is more harmonious? Write down your ideas.

_____

_____

_____

_____

_____

2. During a conversation, your gut might tell you that engaging in a conversation around a potentially polarizing topic would be harmless. In such a situation, what are 3 ways to keep the conversation civilized and avoid unnecessary friction, especially if the other person starts to push back on your perspective on a topic?

_____

_____

_____

_____

_____

3. If the other person triggers a negative emotion in you by bringing up and discussing a particular topic, it's always best to take a few seconds to think about a dignified response that can redirect the conversation. What are 3 things you can do to keep your cool and take a deep breath before responding?

_____

_____

_____

_____

_____

4. Sometimes it's best to let someone know that you feel uncomfortable talking about a topic. Think about 3 ways you can do so in a respectful way (Rule 17). Write down your answers.

_____

_____

_____

_____

_____

5. As you get to know someone more, you'll inevitably talk about all sorts of topics, including difficult ones. Maintaining respect (Rule 17) and having empathy for the other person is critical to fostering and maintaining rapport during such a conversation. What are 3 ways you can increase the likelihood of so maintaining good rapport?

_____

_____

_____

_____

_____

Hit It Off Rule 16 Exercise

Remember the 50/50 Listen/Speak Dynamic in Conversations

Strive for about a 50/50 split during a conversation—you speak 50% of the time and the other person speaks 50% of the time.

Science shows that we tend to violate this rule most of the time; thus, we need to remain mindful of the 50/50 rule.

Use this exercise to train your brain to be more aware of the time split in a conversation so it becomes second nature to allow each person equal time to speak.

1. Have you ever found yourself in conversations where you are speaking too much? Write down how you felt in each case. Were you mindful of how the other person might have felt not getting enough time to participate in the conversation? Did you realize you were dominating the conversation but kept going because it simply felt good?

_____

_____

_____

_____

_____

2. Listening to someone drone on and on is just boring. Think about the last time you were with someone who just kept talking. How did you feel? What was your perception of that person as he or she spoke?

_____

_____

_____

_____

_____

3. Why do you think people (including yourself) like to hear themselves speak? To control a conversation? To steer the topics of conversation? Write down 3 reasons for this impulse we all have from time to time. And then, next to each reason, write down what that reason says about you as a person and measure the answer against how you characterize yourself as a person generally.

_____

_____

_____

_____

_____

4. Not everyone is an extrovert and might desire that you lead, or even dominate, the conversation. Do you know people like this? If so, write their names down and ways you can better involve them in a conversation based on your understanding of the type of person they are.

_____

_____

_____

_____

_____

5. What are your thoughts on politely interrupting someone when they are speaking too much? Do you think this is appropriate? If not, are there times when it might be OK to do so? What about if someone interrupts you? How do you react? Write down your thoughts around interruptions, whether warranted or not.

_____

_____

_____

_____

_____

Hit It Off Rule 17 Exercise

Give Respect to Get Respect

A high level of respect for someone can create a strong connection and lack of respect can kill a relationship.

Science shows that respect is more important to people than how much money they have.

Use this exercise to be more conscious of showing respect to people during your conversations with them, thus acknowledging their value as human beings and honoring them—whether you agree with them or not.

1. You need to respect yourself. Others will observe the level of respect that you have for yourself, and that may drive their decision as to whether you are deserving of their respect. Do you respect yourself? Write down 3 ways you do so.

_____

_____

_____

_____

_____

2. If you allow people to disrespect you, then they'll likely continue to do so. Have you encountered people who have not shown you the respect you deserve? Write down 3 ways they have disrespected you and how you felt when that happened.

_____

_____

_____

_____

_____

3. Always think about how your words and actions will affect others. Have you ever said something that was disrespectful to someone? If so, write down what you said, and ways you could have either said something else more respectful or redirected the conversation into a new direction.

_____

_____

_____

_____

_____

4. Unless necessary (and usually it's not), just let comments go to the wayside instead of saying something that might be considered disrespectful by the other person. It is very tempting to push back if someone says something to you that is disrespectful. It is in our nature to stand up for ourselves. Are there times when pushing back is not warranted given the goal for the overall relationship? If so, write down 3 times when it would be more prudent to let the

disrespectful comment go rather than fight back. But remember you also need to demonstrate respect for yourself in the process.

_____

_____

_____

_____

_____

5. Regular use of the other rules in this book is a demonstration of respect to everyone you meet. Write down 3 of the *21 Rules* in this book that might be most effective in showing respect to others?

_____

_____

_____

_____

_____

Hit It Off Rule 18 Exercise

Say Thanks and Foster Gratitude

Be appreciative of people and say thank you.

Science shows that thanking people strengthens relationships.

Use this exercise to be more effective when you thank someone and remain mindful of the opportunities that arise to show your gratitude.

1. Think about how you felt when someone did *not* thank you for something. Think about 3 times when that happened and write them down and then describe how you felt in each case.

_____

_____

_____

_____

_____

2. Other than saying the words "Thank you," what other ways can you communicate your gratitude for people? Write down 3 ways.

_____

_____

_____

_____

3. When you thank someone, which of the other *21 Rules* might you combine with your thanks to show that person your sincerity and make your words more meaningful. Write down 3 such rules and why combining them with grateful words can be effective.

_____

_____

_____

_____

_____

4. Use other phrases in addition to a direct "Thank you" to create depth to your gratitude (e.g., "I won't forget this." "Truly appreciated." "I wasn't expecting that." "That is very kind of you." "That's really meaningful to me." "How can I return the favor?" "I owe you big time.") Write down 3 other things you can also say in addition to "Thank you."

_____

_____

_____

_____

_____

5. When someone thanks you, of course respond by saying, "You're welcome." But what else can you say or do to add some additional heartfelt gratitude of your own in response? Write down 3 things.

_____

_____

_____

_____

Hit It Off Rule 19 Exercise

Socially Reward Through Your Sincere Praise

Be generous with your compliments of others.

Science shows that praise makes people feel good.

Use this exercise to maximize the powerful scientific effect of praising others.

1. Paying someone a compliment is a great way to break the ice. What are 3 sincere compliments you can pay someone when you first meet that person to set the stage for a mutually rewarding conversation? Write them down.

_____

_____

_____

_____

2. In a romantic relationship, the last thing you want to do is make someone feel uncomfortable by showering too many compliments before you get to know that person. As your familiarity increases, it becomes more appropriate to shower that person with more and

more praise. Write down 3 compliments that you would feel comfortable paying someone earlier in a romantic relationship?

_____

_____

_____

_____

_____

3. Praise people for their successes, showing that you are sincerely impressed with their achievements. Write down 3 ways you can research someone's successes before a scheduled meeting so you are armed with that information and can compliment that person appropriately.

_____

_____

_____

_____

_____

4. When you receive a compliment, remember to always be humble. Write down 3 ways to respond to a compliment in a way that shows your humility.

_____

_____

_____

_____

_____

5. Public praise can be really effective in generating good feelings from the person getting the compliment. Think about the sort of compliments that are best said in private and some that are appropriate to say in front of others. Write them down.

Hit It Off Rule 20 Exercise

Build Rapport
and Reap Relationship Riches

Rapport exists when people feel in sync or are on the same wavelength because they feel similar in some way.

Science shows that we prefer people who we perceive to be like ourselves.

Use this exercise to actively build rapport with people to more effectively communicate and establish trust.

1. Mirroring and matching a person's body language is a way of establishing rapport non-verbally. What type of characteristics of a person's body language might you more consciously observe to then mirror and match appropriately and sincerely? Write down 3 such characteristics.

_____

_____

_____

_____

_____

2. Small talk is a good way to begin building rapport. Write down 3 go-to small talk topics. Then write down questions you can derive from those topics which you can ask the other person in a conversation.

_____

_____

_____

_____

_____

3. Be attentive to the type of person someone is beyond his or her words. The more you get to know that inner person, the better you can naturally mirror and match that individual. Write down 3 ways you can get to know that part of a person not disclosed through words alone.

_____

_____

_____

_____

_____

4. Rapport can be created through shared experiences (e.g., attending a sporting event, concert, conference, or party together). What 3 shared experiences can you propose to people to create a long-lasting positive effect?

_____

_____

_____

_____

5. Have you ever found yourself out of rapport with someone? Write down 3 ways you can attempt to re-establish the rapport you once had. Think about those things that brought you into rapport with the other person in the first place.

_____

_____

_____

_____

_____

Hit It Off Rule 21 Exercise

Gift Positivity
for Positive Results

**Maintain a positive outlook on life and bring your happiness
into your relationships.**

**Science shows that injecting "positive affect"
—essentially happiness—into a relationship increases
the likelihood of making that relationship a success.**

*Use this exercise to more consciously inject happiness into your relationships
to maximize the power of positive affect.*

1. Reflect the characteristics of other happy people you meet. Think about people you know who seem happy. Write down 3 of their characteristics that suggest they are happy people?

_____

_____

_____

_____

_____

2. Strive for an enduring level of happiness by engaging in activities you really enjoy doing. Write down 3 things you very much like doing and think about strategies to do them more.

_____

_____

_____

_____

_____

3. Have you ever found yourself in a conversation that is not upbeat and positive? Think about 3 ways to put a positive spin on those discussions and bring up the emotional tone of the conversation.

_____

_____

_____

_____

_____

4. From time to time we will be in a conversation with someone who seems down in the dumps. What are 3 ways you could help that person—ways to cheer him or her up and direct the conversation into a more positive direction? Write them down.

_____

_____

_____

_____

5. Reciprocally, sometimes we are speaking with someone when we are in a funk. It's better to be honest about how you feel than allow the other person to misinterpret how you feel as somehow his or her fault. Can you think of 3 times when you were in a situation with people and felt down, but did not let them know about how you were feeling? Then write down how you could have let them know and think about how letting them know might have made you feel differently.

_____

_____

_____

_____

_____